NO WAY DUDE
By Jeff Zahorsky

Table of Contents

Foreword

Life is tough, hard and—at times—coldly unforgiving. All of that causes each of us to ask some very hard and direct questions about life, eternity, and *"where am I going after this life?"* In today's world some of the answers to those questions are not all that satisfying, refreshing, or hope-producing. Some of the most compelling questions young people ask today are, *"Is God real?"*, *"Does God really love me?"*, *"Can I be forgiven for all that I've done?"*, *"Is Heaven a reality?"*, and if so, *"How can I get to Heaven?"*

When you pick up this book and start reading, these questions and more are immediately answered. Instantly, you find yourself on an exciting contemporary journey being lead toward an understanding of a new relationship with Christ that will change your life for all of eternity. New knowledge, skills, and abilities are discussed and developed as Christ is introduced into the reality of life's equation. Jeff has detailed each step with precision and accuracy as he leads us through scripture introducing us to timeless truths about knowing God in a very personal way.

When most people speak about or think of Hawaii, some of the first things that come to mind are warm sunny days, palm trees, hula dancers, pineapples, and Waikiki Beach. *Not necessarily a spiritual awakening!* But, over 23 years ago a young Sailor's life was changed forever in a remarkable instant as he came to know Jesus Christ as his personal Lord and Savior. This event took place on the deck of a United States Warship; the USS CHOSIN (CG-65), an Aegis Guided Missile Cruiser home-ported in Pearl Harbor, Hawaii.

Jeff was one of her crewmembers and was searching for meaning in his life and started asking a few questions about his spirituality. I know because I was the one who stood by him as he asked those questions. As a Navy Chaplain, I was empowered by my denomination and the Navy Chaplain Corps to stand with this Sailor to assist him as he searched for answers to some of the spiritual questions and struggles he was experiencing in life. Most importantly, as a man of faith, I was there to assist him in the understanding of what it means *"to come to know Christ in a real and personal way."*

Answering these spiritual questions had significant impact immediately on Jeff's personal life and it ushered in a new understanding of what it means to be free in Christ and to have eternal life. For Jeff Zahorsky, being a Sailor in Hawaii was a life-changing experience that built deep within him an intense love for Christ and a desire to share his faith with others. For the first time in his life, he was free of the shortcomings of life. Jeff was cleansed, forgiven, reconciled, and forever a member of God's family.

"*No Way Dude*" is the fifth book in the series focused on a contemporary mode of evangelism. Jeff's writing style is very attractive and inviting to people living in this time and age. Using vernacular like, *Dude, Dudette, Homie,* and *HomeGirl* creates a comfortable language usage that invites us to speak about spiritual life in ordinary everyday informal speech patterns that communicate God's message clearly to modern generations.

In my *"Evangelism for Chaplains"* course at Columbia International University, I try and lay the foundations for the imperative need of sharing the Gospel message in a clear and concise manner. If we can't tell the story in a clear understandable way, then the people who need to hear the Gospel, which bears the Good News, will never hear the life-saving message of Christ. Jeff does it by first answering the questions that reveal how one can find Heaven.

In this book, Jeff addresses what changes need to be made in your life that produces a *new and abundant life*. It is clearly articulated that when we allow Christ to change us into *His* image, then this new and abundant life that is described is ours. Almost immediately, those around us notice that something has changed, most notably that we have stopped grumbling. What they are noticing is the change in our life, the conversion from the old way of life to the new way of life in and through Jesus Christ. They can see the conversion. Christ makes an instant difference in our life. That is what this author clearly and pointedly identifies as he chronicles the change that Scripture indicates in a relationship with the Son of God.

The best part of the story is the application phase of each chapter. It shows us the *"how to"* in reference to being a follower of Christ. If that is not enough, there is a diagram that is a takeoff of the old Family Feud game called, *"No Way Dude Feud."* Each of the illustrations and diagrams in the latter pages are well done and give a clear and concise explanation of the Gospel message. For all the techno geeks, there are links to web pages, the four other books Jeff has written, and the *nowaydude.org* blog, music, and book updates.

No Way Dude is a must tool for contemporary evangelism. It is clear, concise, and accurate in the presentation of the Gospel message of Jesus Christ. It is a very useful tool in sharing the Gospel with the present generation.

I am thankful for God's blessings. Most of the time Chaplains, Ministers, and Missionaries do not get to see the fruit of their labor. However, in this case, God has blessed me with a million dollar check, in that he has allowed me to see the fruit that He is producing in and through Jeff Zahorsky. I am extremely proud of Jeff and his ministry. Jeff Zahorsky has proven in the series of books he has written that he is a kingdom builder for the King of Kings. For his faith, dedication, and blessing of an old mentor, I am forever thankful.

In the end, *No Way Dude* is hard to put down, not only because of the clear Scriptural guide to Christ, but the even clearer application to how it applies to and is relevant in one's life today. It has purpose, is powerful, and is compellingly told in such a way that lives will be changed for all of eternity.

To God be the glory forever and ever. Amen.

Michael W. Langston, D. Min.
CAPT, CHC, USN, (Ret.)
Professor of Chaplaincy
Columbia International University

Acknowledgments

I would like to start by acknowledging my beautiful and precious wife, Gladys. The list is far too wide and long to note—as to all of the reasons why. For example, if it weren't for her commitment to me, as well as her expert assistance in proofing this book, I'd be in *big trouble!*

I would like to honor my parents, Cheryl and Jerome. Without them, I would not be the person I am, today. My heart is filled with gratitude for their ongoing commitment to me, as a son.

My sister Laurie has always been a voice of encouragement in my life. For this I'm truly blessed and pleased to have her as my sister.

Finally, for every person who has crossed my path and been part of my life—I am *so, so very grateful* because of it. You know who you are! God uses people and situations in our lives to draw us closer to Himself. He is the *Big Idea!* This is why each encounter I have had with these many *unmentioned people*—has been *far from* irrelevant.

For these reasons, understand you have each played a part in the release of this book. Always know my heart is filled with immense gratitude towards you.

Dedication

This book is dedicated to Michael W. Langston.
For being my Andrew. I am forever grateful.

HOW YOU GOT TO HEAVEN

No Way, Dude...

Way!

Introduction

- **Could you be mistaken** about God and the path to Heaven?
- **Is it true** only "good" people make it to Heaven?
- **Can you know for sure** you will make it to Heaven?

All this and much more as we investigate:

NO WAY DUDE
How You Got to Heaven

Hello, Friend. Welcome to *No Way Dude*.

Let me ask you a quick question. When you wake up and get ready for your day, do you *avoid the mirror* or—do you manage to intentionally make your way to it? Why is this?

Oh? You need to handle a few things before facing the day ... and before facing others? It's cool! I totally get it. I'm with you on this.

Keeping this idea in mind, allow me invite you to maintain this *same and appropriate perspective* as you begin to read this book.

"How's that?" you might ask?

Simple. You will most likely have a brief look at what this book is about and decide whether or not you think it's worth your time to purchase and read it. Then at some point, you'll start to discover something. You'll realize there are sections presented as ***bold and italicized*** passages which are cited from the Holy Bible.

My friend, you cannot continue to avoid the Word of God and have life, successfully. This is why God has given us his Word. It's to cut through the darkness and the lies of this existence. I'm begging you right now to put aside any and all of your presuppositions regarding the Bible. Forget about anyone who has offended you in the name of God. You are going to see Bible verses in this book. They are here to act as *your spiritual mirror*, much akin to your current, physical mirrors. Make enough sense to investigate further? *Good!*

As you proceed, I want you to picture avoiding your physical mirror whenever you are inclined to avoid this book entirely or Bible verses in this book, OK?

Ask yourself: What reasonable person continually avoids their physical mirrors? What if your hair is a mess and you have a long, wiry eyebrow hair requiring a snip? How can you see this without a mirror? You can feel it, perhaps. Also, those who are blind may not be able to use a physical mirror.

However, these are the exceptions, not the rule. Right?

Right! So, you're going to head out into public like this, not having checked yourself in the mirror? No grooming? No straightening? The list of examples can go on. You get the picture, though. Right?

Right! Now, what do you immediately think about a person who *does* go out and into their day like this, though? Wouldn't you ask yourself something like, *"Doesn't that person own a mirror? Can't they even see what a mess they are? Don't they own a comb or a brush or something? What are they thinking? I wonder: are they stable? Maybe they are on drugs or have issues or are depressed?"*

OK, so nobody would ever come in the vicinity of thinking something like this. So, I'll claim this spot for sake of illustration. Fair enough? Cool!

So, what is the point? The point is this is how I want you to perceive yourself when—at any juncture—you walk away from either this book, *or*—the **bolded, italicized** verses in this book.

Tell you what. Let's bond and agree on something. There is a limitation on physical life, right? You've probably been to a funeral or two in your time, right? Same here.

We also know there is a *spirit realm* if we are honest with ourselves and others, right? Agreed. See, we agree. This is why I am asking you to allow for yourself to look into the *spiritual mirror* God has given to each of us—as you read this book.

It's all good, trust me. Even though you may not like what you see in the physical mirror many times, you likely appreciate it for the service it provides to you, don't you? It aids you in being able to put your very best foot forward, doesn't it? Of course! And since your soul goes on *forever and ever* but *your body does not,* let's make a decision *today.* Let's make a decision to start paying closer attention to the welfare of our souls, over and above the body. Maintaining your body is important, but we both agree the soul lives on longer than this body, right?

Fantastic! I'm right here with you on this. As a spirit who possesses a body and a *soul (e.g. mind, will & emotions),* you need a mirror even more than your body does, right?

Yes, it's true! So again, don't get all thrown into a panic when you start to see Scripture quotes in this book. They are being presented in order to make sense out of how you got to Heaven, OK? *You're not the person* leaving home all up in a mess, OK? *You're much too sharp* for such foolish behavior; am I right? *You know I'm right! Let's keep on keepin' it real, alright? Cool!*

Quick backdrop. So, now that we've handled some foundational and important business, please allow me to give you a very quick backdrop regarding how this book came to be.

This book was originally projected to be *autobiographical* in order to illustrate the *astonishing* things God has done in my life. He took a hedonistic, spiritually bankrupt soul from the pit of emptiness and placed my feet on solid ground. He anchored my soul forever and ever and you *were going to* hear all about it in this book.

Since then, however … my mind has changed. Perhaps I will get that information out in another book. Perhaps not. As it stands, *this book* concerns *you!* Isn't this more intriguing to you than a book about me? I mean, I could tell you some crazy stories, but really—let's try to keep this as close to a family show as possible, OK?

Rather than conform to what appears to be the norm: *"Enough about you. Let's talk about me!"* Let's instead do it this way: *"Enough about me. Let's talk about you!"*

I've been assigned to a mission and it includes you. *Yeah, you!* You have a front row seat to God's plan in this book. This isn't the fake pop-religion you are accustomed to. This is the narrow stuff. It stands out from the rest of the world. Oftentimes, it's severely misunderstood. Nevertheless, it's true through and through.

You heard correctly. It's not a popular thing. *Religion* might be *popular*, but *this isn't religion*. Religion can't get you to Heaven. Religion is man's attempt to reach God on his own. You can't make it to Heaven like this. God must reach down to you and take you to Heaven, OK? There's no other way. A perfect, Holy God and—a dirty, sinful person is just going to reach right up and get into Heaven?

Some may say, *"I can!"* Really? Show me! You can't do it. Nobody can do this. They'd be incinerated by the glorious light of the living God, right? *Poof!*

God must make a way and ... He has. It's *His way,* though. Not anybody else's way. His way and His alone. We're going to get to this *way*, soon enough.

Ready? I know you are! Now, one must be determined to *peel back the layers* in order to see what is inside a thing; wouldn't you agree?

For example, how many counterfeits of various things are out there? You know what I mean, right? *Knock-offs* of the *real thing?*

You see, when something is counterfeited it's typically because it has some type of *value.* If fancy cell phones and money are counterfeited, imagine what is going on with *eternal truth* from generation to generation. Imagine what is going on with the answer as to how a person can *inherit eternal life. "If ..."* of course they will say, *"...there **is** an afterlife."*

My friend, I realize there's a good chance we have yet to meet. You are still my friend, though ... because God has demonstrated: love is a *choice*; love is a *verb*. I choose to call you friend because God has created you for a special purpose. He has commissioned me to tell you all about it. This is how the Spirit of God moves! The purpose for this book is for you to know and enjoy your Creator in a lasting, meaningful, love relationship.

It's a two-way street when it comes to love. Love requires a response. God has reached down from heaven to demonstrate his love for you. This is what we are going to discuss because it all has to do with: *How You Got to Heaven!*

We have to peel back some layers.

Are you ready to get started? Personally, I cannot wait.

Let's jump into this thing, then ... right now. *Vamonos! (Let's go!)*

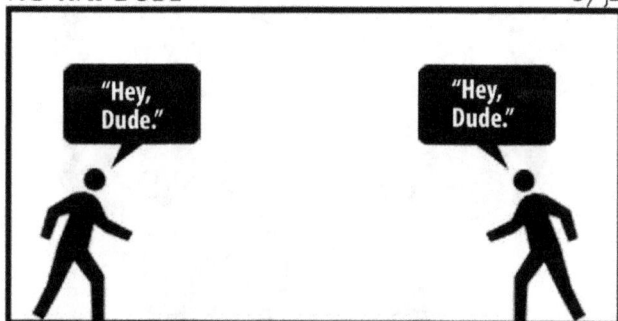

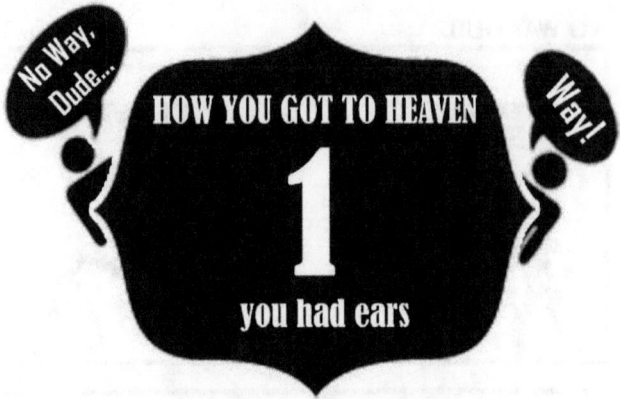

How Did You Get To Heaven?
YOU HAD EARS

To Hear

Regardless of what society may be telling you, eternal, flawless truth has revealed you have a terrible cancer. *Whoa!* You didn't know this was going to be the *No Way Dude* moment right off the bat; did ya? *Oh yeah! It's on and it's all true, my friend!*

This cancer you have is *sin*. Sin dwells in your members. You were born with it and those who aren't telling you about it are likely not qualified to do so—anyhow. So, why are you listening to them? Do you call a plumber when you need your car repaired? *C'mon, now!*

This is your soul we are talking about. This is *Heaven and Hell* stuff, *Gambler! Don't bust out.* Are you going to trust unqualified people, the mockers and the scoffers or even churches which conflict or confuse God's truth? Or, are you going to listen to God?

Well, the Creator strikes me as pretty qualified to talk on the matter and *He lives in me,* so let's stop playing games, already. Life is short! You gotta get this right and we're gonna get you there with *No Way Dude.* Trust me. God is going to *so spin your head with his love*—you might eventually be inclined to repeat this book title to yourself, alright? I'm serious. Let's go.

Now, let's say a woman who doesn't know she has breast cancer goes to see her doctor. She goes to a doctor and the doctor either doesn't detect her cancer or—he doesn't tell her about it.

Good doctor? Fine ambassador for the medical profession? No way! Take that Dude's license away, right?

Well, God has graced me to be used by Him to help you out. I'm not going to be that irresponsible doctor or shameful ambassador. Rather, I'm going to do my job. You likely were not aware of when your dentist or doctor was going to school and getting qualified to ultimately treat you, right?

In a similar way, you were not with me during my struggles in life and when God ultimately qualified me to speak to your issue of sin today, right? Some who even think they may know me—because of knowing me in previous times—could have a *limited* understanding of who I really am as well, right? People don't always understand *you*, do they? Or, who *you* really are, right?

Even people who *think* they know another oftentimes get it wrong, don't they?

The parents of the deceased son say, *"I never thought sweet Cindy would feed poor Jim cyanide to poison him for the life insurance money. Boy, did we have her pegged wrongly."*

So you see, we can get it wrong at times. *Oftentimes*, actually; right? Many people think someone has to be wearing a Pope's hat or a white collar to teach them anything about God. When actually, Jesus greatly criticized the religious, *holier-than-thou* leaders as *vipers* and *children of the evil one*. What matters when it comes to God's truth isn't so much what a person is wearing on the outside. Rather, it's whether or not a person actually has *Jesus inside*. Are you with me? *I told you it was on* and *Jesus wants out*. So, let's continue!

As previously indicated, you have a wicked, condemning cancer called sin within your members. The bigger problem is you don't have the power to overcome this disease on your own. Sin has a power way too strong for the spiritually dead person to overcome. Dead people need life, which is why we're having this discussion. One cannot just declare, *"I'm spiritually alive!"* It's great to have zeal, but it must be according to knowledge. Knowledge of the truth.

With most people having both of their physical ears in place, it's an amazing thing so many still don't seem to hear the most important message ever revealed. This is because in a mysterious but very real way, only God can draw a soul to his Truth; God the Son. According to Jesus, we read:

Jesus said to him, "I am the way, and the truth, and the life; no one comes to the Father but through Me.
—John 14:6 NASB

"No one can come to Me unless the Father who sent Me draws him; and I will raise him up on the last day."
—John 6:44 NASB

Then he said, "I tell you the truth, unless you turn from your sins and become like little children, you will never get into the Kingdom of Heaven."
—Matthew 18:3 NLT

If you do some research, you will find that possibly the most loved and hated Man of all time—Jesus Christ—gives us some insight about human beings. Why do people quote Jesus? It's because Jesus is a Man of tremendous credibility; isn't He? Our calendar pivots upon of his very life; **B.C. / A.D.** *(Before Christ, Ano Domini, "The year of our Lord.")*

Jesus made some comments about *hearing*, as well as *having ears*. We read, again:

> **"This is why I speak to them in parables: Though seeing, they do not see; though hearing, they do not hear or understand."**
> —Matthew 13:13 NIV
>
> ###
>
> **Then he said, "Anyone with ears to hear should listen and understand."**
> —Mark 4:19 NLT

When it comes to going to Heaven, everybody has opinions, but Jesus weighs in firmly and says: *"I tell you the truth!"*

Why then do so many people get caught up accepting the wrong message when it comes to Heaven? Why are so many *religious* people *(wearing fancy robes or not)* in such great error when it comes to properly understanding how to get to Heaven?

You remember Nicodemus, right? He was a *religious* guy, right? Israel's *teacher*. Nic likely wore religious garb. However, it might be helpful to keep in mind: *common folk* are often still trapped by religion, as well. *Religion* is man's *attempt* to reach the infinitely, holy God of the Universe. The only problem with this is: man reaching his highest is unable to reach God. God *must reach down to you* and He has, in Jesus.

But, I digress. Back to Nicodemus!

Even Nicodemus—with all of his religious influence—appeared to be somewhat confused over the message Jesus delivered to him. Let's listen in on some of what was said during this *Nic@night* encounter:

Jesus answered and said to him, "Truly, truly, I say to you, unless one is born again he cannot see the kingdom of God."

Nicodemus said to Him, "How can a man be born when he is old? He cannot enter a second time into his mother's womb and be born, can he?" Jesus answered, "Truly, truly, I say to you, unless one is born of water and the Spirit he cannot enter into the kingdom of God. That which is born of the flesh is flesh, and that which is born of the Spirit is spirit. Do not be amazed that I said to you, '<u>You must be born again.</u>' The wind blows where it wishes and you hear the sound of it, but do not know where it comes from and where it is going; so is everyone who is born of the Spirit."

Nicodemus said to Him, "How can these things be?" Jesus answered and said to him, "Are you the teacher of Israel and do not understand these things?"
—John 3:3-10 NASB

Did you notice this? Even Nicodemus was struggling with the truth of God and he was *supposed to be teaching others* about God.

Let this encourage you!

Simultaneously, let it serve as a warning as to how the truth of God—and going to *heaven* instead of *hell*—is not to be glossed over with assumptions. Nor, should it be taken casually.

God has made the way to Heaven *narrow*. The way into this physical world was narrow *(i.e. your mother's womb);* right?

Likewise, the way into God's spiritual family is *also* narrow. Why is this a surprise to people? You are on your way down this narrow road because we're gonna do this thing, OK? Let's do it, *together!*

The Word of Christ. Just as any loving parent is concerned with the safety of their child or children, so the Father of spirits is concerned with the safety of *his* children.

The issue at hand, however, is one first needs to make sure they are God's child. This is how God cares for his children—by the very act of making them or *adopting* them as his very own child.

So, how does God—the Father of spirits—look out for the safety of his children? He does this by offering them salvation while lost and in an *orphaned* state. Salvation is to be saved or *safe* from condemnation, which is an eternity separated from God. It's good news but you first have to grab it for it to matter in your life. Do you collect your two hundred bucks before or after you pass *Go? Who puts the cart before the horse?*

So it is with salvation. You must first become God's child before you can gain his promises and eternal inheritance. It starts now, not later!

Look. Think. It's clear. There's only *one* way into a saving relationship with God:

***Jesus said to him, "I am the way, and the
truth, and the life; no one comes to the
Father but through Me."***
—John 14:6 NASB

God is going to show you his love throughout
this book by pouring eternal truth into your life.
People talk about *love* this and *love* that. Exactly!
Love. And do you know what? *Love* rejoices in
the *truth*. The truth is, the *world* doesn't know
what love is—but *God does* because ... why? *It's
because God is love!*

Who can really say God is love and have
proof? The Christ-follower can. Why, again?
Well, who actually proved it? Correct! *God
proved it* in sending Jesus, God the Son, to shed
his blood on the Cross for you. What kind of love
is this? *Amazing, unspeakable love* is what it is!
Who's laying their life down for you? Who's
offering you the real happily-ever-after? I'm
waiting. *They* control eternity and Heaven and
Hell? No way! Jesus does though, and He's ready
to take you into eternal bliss with Him if you'll
only have ears to hear. Can ya do it? *Of course
you can!*

So again, understand the Father of spirits
wants to save you through his *only* and *perfect*
provision. He also wants to then guide you or
lead you with his eye, as it were.

For example, you know what wild animals are like, right? They run around all crazy and so forth. Take dogs or horses, for instance. They both need to be broken in or trained, don't they? People may want to argue this but if it was all about them running around free without any type of discipline or guidance—you know there'd be trouble. Am I wrong?

Dogs will run your house if you don't—out of *love and common sense—train them.* Right? If not, why the dog training? Why the TV shows?

Then you have the horses. Those things need to be broken in and trained up, don't they? Wild horses and so-called freedom? Hey, I get the beauty of seeing and allowing these awesome creatures to run around in the open field. I get that. But, you know as well as I do there is something necessary and loving about training and leading these animals, right?

Well, what about children? Children are not animals, contrary to popular teaching. *(Take about 30 minutes of well spent time to see Evolution vs. God on YouTube at your earliest opportunity!)*

Even so, children need to be trained up, don't they? If not, why the parent to child corrections? Why the, *"Don't you talk back to me!"* stuff? Why the, *"It's time for bed."* commands? Why the guidance and leadership from the parent, where good and proper parenting exists?

It's because it makes sense. It's because God has been a loving Father forever and He came up with the whole parenting thing in the first place.

This is why God's heart is to save you and guide you. You cannot have this without a relationship, first. This is why you need to have a new birth by being adopted into his family, through Jesus. Not church, Jesus.

Additionally, this is why once God saves you, His will and perfect plan is to lovingly discipline and guide you home through the reading and hearing of his Word, the Holy Bible. God has given you a love letter in the Holy Bible. He wants to *guide you with his eye*, not yank you or jerk you like a dog on a chain or a wild horse—by bit and bridle.

> **"Do not be like a senseless horse or mule that needs a bit and bridle to keep it under control."**
> —Psalms 32:9 NLT

The exhortations of this book. So, as we close out this first chapter, you need to know I'm *really, really, really* here to show you *How You Got To Heaven*. It's not burdensome to me. I'm very pleased to be like one of those guys who used to carry messages before modern communications.

Apparently, when the King or someone was waiting upon an answer to a specific message, the *look-out* person would be able to see the messenger from a long ways off.

Before they could ever *hear* them, they could *see* them. To draw an inference regarding the likely answer, the look-out would assess the messenger's demeanor. It was oftentimes based upon <u>how they were running</u> and the <u>position of their head</u> *(i.e. was their head hanging and feet dragging? Or—were they excited and hurrying excitedly about!)*

What does God have to say about the message I am bringing to you, today? Let's look:

"How beautiful are the feet of messengers who bring good news!"
—Romans 10:15

Another thing I'd invite you to think about is: How much greater than an earthy parent is the Father of spirits?

An earthly, loving parent *loves, disciplines and guides their child, right? Absolutely.* What about God, the Father of spirits?

Well, His will is for you to be saved from damnation. This is why He became a Man. In doing so, he sent His one and only *begotten Son* to make a way for your escape.

You see, God oftentimes uses *unlikely* vessels to carry and share this amazing message of His love for you. It's a message many consider to be foolishness, only because it is they who are perishing. We read:

> *"Instead, God chose things the world considers foolish in order to shame those who think they are wise. And he chose things that are powerless to shame those who are powerful."*
> —1 Corinthians 1:27 NLT

Like me, you know what it is to be perishing. It's to be detached from the love of God, most likely because of pride. Detached also perhaps due to a *religious spirit* and certainly—an unregenerate heart.

In reading this book and allowing bits of God's Word to fall into any good soil available in your heart, God is ministering his saving peace and love directly to you. You need only to continue to receive His counsel.

God's Holy Spirit will guide and direct you into all peace and safety. Not peace and safety as the world promises, but peace and safety as He promises.

For, in the leaving of the empty tomb, God has defeated the World and death. He wants you to have this victory. The way to have this victory is to invite Him in. Then and only then, can you be victorious and begin to fight *from* a place of victory; *not for it.*

The battle has been won. Are you going to be *more than a conqueror?* I know you are, so let's watch it happen. God is amazing!

Summary

There's always a price to pay when we don't have ears to hear the truth, right? The person driving the car ends up lost, but pride prevents them from seeking out and benefiting from the truth. Isn't this how it goes during those awkward situations?

The reason you ended up getting into Heaven is because you stopped to ask for directions, though. I just know it! God is already pouring truth into your heart. You are more aware of consequences of various things. You are more aware God is attempting to get your attention.

In this short time, God has touched a place deep within you that only He can satisfy. He placed eternity in your heart[i] and only He can fill it. This is why you are ready and willing to dive deeper into these coming chapters. It's because the things of this world always over-promise and under-deliver. You want more and God couldn't be more pleased you are seeking out how you got to Heaven.

Do you know why? I think you know why. It's because it involves an eternally satisfying relationship with Him. We're just getting started. Strap yourself in because God is going to take you places where you have never been.

Life Application

1. How long have you been searching for Heaven? Did you always know it had to do with God, the Creator of the Universe? Or, did you think it didn't involve a "God?"

2. Have you historically been a person who has given attention to spiritual matters? Or, have you typically closed your mind off to such things? In what way do you think this helps or hinders you in reading a book such as this?

3. Do you think it's possible to hear *without* your physical ears? If so, what part of your overall make-up do you think can also *hear?*

No Way, Dude...

Way!

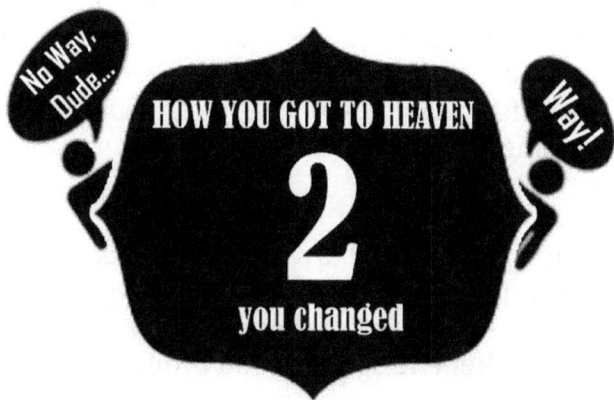

How Did You Get To Heaven?
YOU CHANGED

Your Mind

About God's Word. *"Aw,"* she said with a smile. *"He hasn't changed one bit. He's still the same!"*

The same old so and so? Contrary to popular belief, this is *never* a positive thing unless, that is—a person has been born twice.

Some will say, *"Never change! Don't you ever change!"* —as if this is some type of great quality to possess.

No, my friend. This is a lie. Either you *ought* to change or you *ought not* to change. Under no circumstance can both be true at the same time, in the same sense.

Therefore, *should* you change or *should you not* change? *Must* you change or *must you not* change?

How did you get to Heaven? You *changed your mind about changing*. You changed your *mind* and your *direction*. In other words, you *repented*. Repenting[ii] is a good thing!

"The times of ignorance God overlooked, but now he commands all people everywhere to repent, because he has fixed a day on which he will judge the world in righteousness by a man whom he has appointed; and of this he has given assurance to all by raising him from the dead."
—Acts 17:30,31 ESV

What is God—through Paul—revealing to you through this passage? He's actually revealing another truth as to how you got to Heaven! That's right! God knew you would get this message, today!

Your Creator revealed a few thousand years ago to Greek men in Athens—once again, using Paul—that God isn't a God who lives in Temples made by man. Rather, He justly expects people to know the truth. He is Spirit and dwells in those human beings who receive Jesus into their heart as Savior and Lord. It's right there, go ahead and read it, again. The way of salvation is not religion, my friend. It's an intimate relationship with God—*who is Spirit*—by answering the door of your heart where Jesus stands and knocks. There is only one way to open it and it's from the inside. This is you!

"Behold, I stand at the door and knock; if anyone hears My voice and opens the door, I will come in to him and will dine with him, and he with Me."
—Revelation 3:20 NASB

So, this is part of how you got to heaven. A big part! These are all *big parts!* Nobody will be in Heaven without having changed their mind—starting at some specific point in time—about God and his truth. It's impossible otherwise because every child born after Adam sinned in the Garden is infected with sin. More than one verse in the Bible reveals this foundational truth to us. I mean, think about. If such were not the case, then why did God wrap himself in human flesh by coming down here to deal with it? *Emmanuel:* God with us, right?

Understand, this tragic position requires a new birth. In order to realize this new birth, God must supernaturally open a person's spiritual eyes as to their desperate need for a Savior and his unique forgiveness. This is exactly what He is doing right now with you! God is good and has chosen the preaching of his truth by his very own clay vessels to do the job. This is Christianity! This is the unique, singular way to Heaven! Surrendered vessels saying, *"I get it, God. I receive You, Jesus. Come into my heart, God. Live in me, fellowship with me. Save me and use me for your glory, Heavenly Father."*

This is what it's all about. Not, *"Oh, I went to church."* Or, *"I gave to charity, so God will let me into Heaven."*

No my friend! Isn't this good news? It's not all about your performance. In this life of yours, it was never all about your performance. The world may play this game with you. Religion may try to play this game with you. God, however, is not playing this game with you. God isn't playing any games at all. Simply look at the Cross of Jesus, his precious and only begotten Son.

Understand: Jesus loved you so much He came to *make a way for you!* It's always been about Jesus! *You are the object of his affection, though!* It's only when God helps you to see this—by his eternal Word—that you begin to realize who God is. Then, the love you experience by receiving what God has done in Jesus releases you from bondage. The bondage of being the lord of your own life; a *god* unto yourself. You were never meant to rule your own life. God is your Ruler. He is your Heavenly Father and He knows perfectly what is best for you.

This is how you got to heaven! God opened your eyes and you made the choice to receive Jesus into your heart. Your Father drew you to his Son so that you would finally have a loving relationship with your only, really true Father. God is the Father of spirits. He is the Giver of life; your life. He was your Papa long before anyone walked this planet and He continues to be as He opens your eyes to exactly who He is. Jesus said:

Jesus said to him, "Have I been with you so long, and you still do not know me, Philip? Whoever has seen me has seen the Father. How can you say, 'Show us the Father'?
—John 14:9 ESV

Keep also in mind this fact: Do not let doubt and fear have any place. Just because you know people have died for Christ's sake *(i.e. martyred)* doesn't mean God doesn't know what is good for you.

For example, is every person who is raped, murdered, tortured (and the like) following Jesus as a Christian; a born-again believer? Of course not. We live in a fallen world, as you have hopefully realized. Spouses are being murdered for life insurance payouts, right? There's a lust for money, a lust for sex and a pride for life ruining lives today. God has better for you along your way to Heaven!

These are just some reasons why God is commanding you to change your mind and your direction. Heaven is one, narrow way. Hell is another, broad way. Many take the broad way but God is revealing to you, today—how you altered course and made an escape.

God is Spirit. By calling upon Jesus to save you by inviting Him into your heart to be your Good Shepherd, you invite in the living God to lead you on home and into Heaven. It's for real. *Let's goooo!*

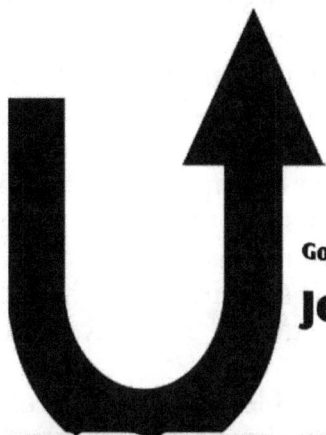

My will
Sin

God's will
Jesus

REPENT
"Change Your Mind"

Repent and turn to God, so that
your sins may be wiped out.
Acts: 3:19

You changed your mind about God's Word: The Holy Bible. There are *many-a-critic* in today's culture when it comes to the Holy Bible. Could it be at least on the table that by default, man is in rebellion to God and his holy standards? This is at least on the table in the marketplace of ideas, isn't it?

I mean, for example: How do most people feel about sex outside of marriage? Teens, adults ... our population, in general? Most people don't have an issue sleeping with whom they want, when they want; do they? My point is simply the following:

The Holy Bible claims to be breathed out by God, through chosen, holy men of God. Forgiven *sinners*, made *sons*. In the Bible, you'll see it clearly stated sex outside of marriage is a crime against God and his moral standard for mankind. God is the Moral Law-Giver, as it were. He sets the standards on morality. Consider the 10 Commandments. So, back to the point.

"Or do you not know that the unrighteous will not inherit the kingdom of God? Do not be deceived; neither fornicators, nor idolaters, nor adulterers, nor effeminate, nor homosexuals, nor thieves, nor the covetous, nor drunkards, nor revilers, nor swindlers, will inherit the kingdom of God."
—1 Corinthians 6: 9, 10 NASB

"Outside the city are the dogs—the sorcerers, the sexually immoral, the murderers, the idol worshipers, and all <u>who love to live a lie.</u>"
—Revelation 22:15 NLT

The point is the Bible reveals and claims to be God's eternal Word. By the very fact God says sex outside of marriage is w-r-o-n-g, then the masses dismiss this and do what their sinful hearts desire—proves as just one example—man is *by default* in disagreement with God on the sex thing. Is this a fair assessment?

Therefore, I'm simply and only trying to demonstrate we have a conflict between God's Word and man, in pop culture. The Bible is at the center of this because it acts as a mirror into the very center of man's spirit. With this being the case, is it any wonder pop culture attempts to shoot down the very thing which reveals God's heart and eternal truth? We read:

"The grass withers and the flowers fall, but the word of our God endures forever."
—Isaiah 40:8 NIV

There are so many verses I can share with you to demonstrate the eternal importance of discovering, submitting to and being transformed by God's eternal Word. Let's scope out a few of them so you can *get some confidence going* in the right direction. It's the direction of *eternal truth* and the foundation you base it upon is critical.

By the way, this isn't *sub*jective; this is *ob*jective. Either a thing is right or wrong, but under no circumstance can it be both at the same time, in the same sense. This would be a contradiction. Either God is capable of revealing his eternal truth using men to pen it, or He isn't. If God can speak stars into place and call them each by name, is He not able to convey his Word?

Of course He is and He *has* done it! Stop paying attention to the Bible nay-sayers and get on board with God. His wisdom is not man's wisdom and He uses the foolish things of this world to confound the wise. Stop worrying about what other people are doing and lock into what *God* is saying and doing. He'll never let you down and He's got it all covered in his Word.

Now, before we dig deeper into how you are going to end up in Heaven, let's first observe some things.

What are a few reasons why *accepting* and *digesting* truth appears to be such a difficult task for people, in general?

One major issue we won't get into right now is because there is a powerful, spiritual being attempting to take you out. By showing you how you got to Heaven, the victory will become yours.

The other issue is that, according to God:

Human beings—his very own creation— are *estranged* from their mother's womb.[iii] Since the *Creator* has never needed the *created* to define who *He* is and what *He* is like (as well as who *they* are and what *they* are like), God has revealed Himself and the truth about matters in various ways.

Your Creator has used people and continues to use people to communicate his message. At the same time, He has orchestrated the *capturing of* his eternal truth in writing. He has used these very same people—his creation—to record this truth.

It's all done. The Book—the Holy Bible—is written and has been written for quite some time, now. A few thousand years, actually. It's the best-selling book of all time.[iv] So much so, the charts stopped listing it!

I can just imagine the chatter: *"What is the #1 Best Seller? Oh man, it's the Holy Bible. Not again! Let's just stop listing it."*

There's no adding to it and there's no taking away from it—for those who desire to be on the side of God. God does as He pleases. He's God, right? He's the Potter, we are the clay.

We won't have time to get into the landslide of evidence we have for the Holy Bible being in fact, God's eternal Word. However, what we can do is observe several verses, briefly. You can stand firmly upon these as we touch upon the points being brought out in this book.

"How sweet your words taste to me; they are sweeter than honey."
—Psalms 119:103 NLT

"Your word is a lamp to guide my feet and a light for my path."
—Psalms 119:105 NLT

"Meanwhile, I will tell you what is written in the <u>Book of Truth.</u>"
—Daniel 10:21 NLT

"The sum of <u>your word is truth</u>,"
—Psalm 119:160 ESV

"Of his own will he brought us forth by <u>the word of truth</u>, that we should be a kind of firstfruits of his creatures."
—James 1:18 ESV

"In him you also, when you heard the <u>word of truth</u>, the gospel of your salvation,"
—Ephesians 1:13-14 ESV

*"**All Scripture** is **breathed out by God** and profitable for teaching, for reproof, for correction, and for training in righteousness,"*
—2 Timothy 3:16 ESV

*"... for You have exalted above all else Your name and Your word and **You have magnified Your word above all Your name!**"*
—Psalms 138:2 AMP

"Your word, O LORD, is eternal; it stands firm in the heavens. 90 Your faithfulness continues through all generations; you established the earth, and it endures."
—Psalms 119 NIV

*"Sanctify them in **the truth**; **Your word is truth.**"*
—John 17:17

Some may say, *"I never saw it this way."*

Might I invite you to change your mind? Wise, reasonable people have a change of mind when it makes good sense to do so; don't they? This is indeed one of those cases, I can promise you.

It is God's Word which *converts*, or changes the soul *(i.e. your mind, will and emotions)*. I am speaking spirit, life and truth to you because God's Word is spirit, life and truth. If you were good enough on your own merit, you wouldn't need saving and you wouldn't need God's Word and Spirit to change you.

As it is, God knows you need all of this. This is why He is lovingly confronting you. Without His Spirit and without His Word, you remain hopelessly degenerate and unchanged and wicked. Right, Jesus is the standard and compared to and without God or Jesus, a person is *wicked* in God's eyes. Crazy, right? Crazy perhaps, but true my friend!

Man has a much lower threshold for what true *goodness* is. God is *holy* and *perfect*. He is *light*, in Him is *no darkness at all*. (God desires for you to be good, but without the Spirit of Christ, you will never be categorized as *good* by God. With Jesus, Jesus is all *perfect and good*, and this has all to do with not only being *good,* but also: *How You Got To Heaven!)*

Therefore, wrapping up this portion regarding God's Word, God has a few verses for this one, as well *(e.g. trusting his Word)*. Why? It's because I have already shared with you, *He has it all covered in his Word!* Check it out:

"Do I take any pleasure in the death of the wicked?" declares the Sovereign LORD. "Rather, am I not pleased when they turn from their ways and live?"

—Ezekiel 18:23 NIV

"The Lord isn't really being slow about his promise, as some people think. No, he is being patient for your sake. He does not want anyone to be destroyed, but wants everyone to repent."
—2 Peter 3:9 NLT

Repent? Yes. *Change your mind and direction* when it comes to God's Word. At one time you didn't give it much weight. Currently, however, God is revealing eternal truth to you and lovingly encouraging you to reconsider his Word. He wants you to take special note of how critical and special his Word is intended to be, specifically for you—as well as *for a time such as this.*

About who Jesus is. This one is slightly tricky because the only *complete* way to know who Jesus is—is to give your life to Him. To trust Him. When you do this, you find your way to the Father by the power of the Holy Spirit. Once you begin your love relationship with God, the more you will come to know who Jesus *really* is. God is now beginning to reveal the real Jesus, the *empty-tomb Jesus* ... to you, in the pages of this book. If you really want to know who Jesus is, which is of paramount importance regarding *How You Got to Heaven*, open your heart as you read. You are in a safe place, now. God is dealing with you and his intentions are always pure and lovely. He has a lot to reveal to you and we're going to plunge back into it, right now. Let's go.

First, some may ask, *"What's the big deal about Jesus? He was just a man."*

Or, *"Jesus is just a great teacher. I like Jesus, but I'm not going to worship him!"*

What is the big deal about Jesus? This is one you're going to get correct because you need this one for us to get you home. Let's do a quick check-in with Jesus to get it straight from Him:

"Therefore I said to you that you will die in your sins; for unless you believe that I am He, you will die in your sins."
—John 8:24 NASB

What is Jesus talking about? Friend, don't ever let anyone fool you with any talk about Jesus not being God in the flesh and your only way of salvation. You have to get this one right and you're going to get it right, as promised.

Father, I pray You continue to penetrate this open heart as You continue to reveal your astonishing truth—in Christ's name, Amen!

Jesus has not left you but three options, according to the late, great and brilliant C.S. Lewis. Jesus is only **Liar, Lunatic, or Lord.** Remember this phrase. You must choose. Consider Him a demon from the pits of hell for lying about who He is, consider Him some type of whack nut-job *(by the way, these are my colorful descriptions, not Lewis.')*, OR, call Him Lord and fall at his precious feet and worship Him. Under no circumstance say He was just a great teacher or nice person. Jesus has *not* left you those options.

Jesus claimed to be God *many times* and in *many ways.*[v] I have a list of at least a dozen in the Resources section at the end of this book. For now and for the sake of brevity, I'll supply you with just a few so we can keep pressing forward and get you seated with Christ in the *heavenlies*, all before you even leave this earth!

Did Jesus ever claim to be God? Let's take a peek:

"For <u>I have come down from heaven</u>, not to do My own will, but the will of Him who sent Me."
—John 6:38

###

Therefore the Jews were grumbling about Him, because He said, "I am the bread that came down out of heaven." They were saying, "Is not this Jesus, the son of Joseph, whose father and mother we know? How does He now say, 'I have come down out of heaven'?"
—John 6:41-42

###

Therefore many of His disciples, when they heard this said, "This is a difficult statement; who can listen to it?"
—John 6:60,66

###

"you, a mere man, <u>claim to be God.</u>"
—John 10:33

###

"Yes, <u>I am the bread of life!</u>"
—John 6:48 NLT

###

Jesus said to him, "Have I been so long with you, and yet you have not come to know Me, Philip? He who has <u>seen Me has seen the Father</u>; how can you say, 'Show us the Father '?"
—John 14:9 NASB

# # #

Jesus answered, "I tell you the truth, before Abraham was even born, <u>I Am!</u>"
—John 8:58 NLT

# # #

"<u>All things have been handed over to me by my Father</u>, and no one knows who the Son is except the Father, <u>or who the Father is except the Son and anyone to whom the Son chooses to reveal him.</u>"
—Luke 10:22 ESV

# # #

Jesus said to him, "<u>I am the way, and the truth, and the life</u>; no one comes to the Father <u>but through Me.</u>"
—John 14:6 NASB

Now, don't forget what Jesus said in that first verse above all of these other verses. He gave clear instruction if a person didn't *"believe I am He,"* they'd die in their sins. *"He"* is *God*, right?

"In the beginning was the Word, and <u>the Word was with God, and the Word was God</u>. He was with God in the beginning. <u>Through him</u> all things were made; <u>without him nothing was made</u> that has been made. In him was life, and that life was the light of all mankind."
—John 1:1-4 NIV

###

"So <u>the Word became human</u> and made his home among us. He was full of unfailing love and faithfulness. And we have seen his glory, the glory of the Father's one and only Son."
—John 1:14 NLT

###

"The woman said unto him, I know that Messiah comes, who is called Christ: when he comes, he will tell us all things."

Jesus said unto her, "<u>I</u> that speak unto you <u>am he.</u>"
—John 4:25,26

We just saw only a few but very convincing statements of Jesus claiming to be God. He certainly believes He is God and made many claims surrounding it and gave many convincing proofs. He performed miracles, not the least of which was predicting his own crucifixion and resurrection, only for these things to be recorded in history with evidence of an empty tomb. *Jesus ain't playin'!* He's God and He came to rescue you. You OK? C'mon, we're into it now. *Let's keep this thing goin'!*

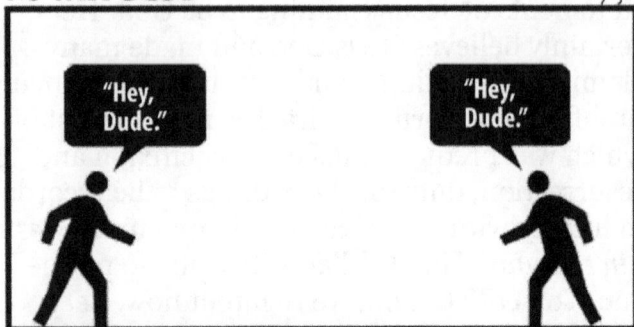

About how much *weight* you *must* apply. God's salvation is based upon *trust*. This is *his* plan. He is perfect and always does everything just right. In order to get you home, we have to make sure you get this part right! Everything hinges upon this one little 5-letter word: *trust*. Another little 5-letter word contends to keep you from it, though: *pride. Yuk!* This isn't going to happen though, right? This book is about how you *got to Heaven*, not how you *didn't get to Heaven;* right?

Therefore, you must apply your *full weight*, your *full trust in Christ*—in order to be saved. Faith equals trust and it's only *by* God's free gift of grace *through faith* by which you can be saved. *Faith ain't no joke, yo!*

When I was a kid attending Roman Catholic grade school, I used to get my new religion book every year as I climbed the ladder towards junior high (or grades *six through nine,* as it were). Yeah. I would see the word, *"Faith"* on the cover or a page inside the book and ask myself, *"What is faith?"* Soon, I learned faith simply meant to *believe*.

But oh, my friend! Do you know what *believe* means in the original? Believe in the original language means *to trust.*[vi] This took me years to discover and I can promise you, it wasn't because I gave my life to Jesus and *stopped seeking*. Sure, *God was the One* reaching out through surrendered vessels placing truth into my path. Without the Lord, where would any of us be?

However, once God starts dealing with you like He is right now, it's *your* job to embrace Him and the truth He is revealing to you.

For me, casually dismissing the words *faith* and *belief* at an early age put me on a rapid path to destruction. My friend, it doesn't matter if you are:

1) **Hootin' it up,** living *La Vida Loca*—doing bombs and belly shots, or ...
2) **An elderly lady** playing bingo or baking apple pies for the coming bake sale, or ...
3) **A soccer Mom,** or ...
4) **A crossing guard,** or ...
5) **The average person** who works hard and generally considers themselves to be pretty good when compared to others.

If the condition of a person lacks *saving faith (trust in Jesus Christ completely)*—it's all just *cuts* in the line to hell. *(Do you remember cutting in line, maybe even on the road?)* Yeah! Here, it's *cuts* in the *line to hell* I'm talking about. You need people in your life speaking the truth to you, not just so-called *friends* tickling your ears when the water temperature is increasing. You heard about the *vacationing frog*, right?

In the case you have not, there was once upon a time a frog. Once upon a time Mr. Frog *loved* back-floating in the water. On this day however, Mr. Frog was snatched up and brought to somebody's house. You remember catching frogs as a kid, maybe?

Yeah. So, in this house, Mr. Frog was gently placed into a pot of nice, cold water. The first problem for Mr. Frog though was … the pot of cold water was sitting on the stove. The *next* problem Mr. Frog had was someone had actually turned the burner on just below the pot!

Even still, Mr. Frog had *already taken to* his water re-entry. So, here's Mr. Frog with his hands behind his head. He's back-stroking around, whistling, blowing bubbles into the air and so forth. He's having a fantabulous time.

Even as the water temperature began to increase, Mr. Frog thought he had died and gone to Heaven. We listen in:

"What amazing weather we are having today. This new place is like a Jacuzzi in paradise!"

But oh my friend, Mr. Frog's next and biggest *issue* was—the water was coming to a rapid boil. Mr. Frog had the slightest clue as to what was coming!

This *gaining cuts in the line to hell* isn't you, though. Remember? This is about *how you got to Heaven*. So, let's use this as a springboard to catapult you onto the narrow and exclusive road to Heaven. The last thing you need in your journey is some false hope stating,

"All is well. I am going to back-float into Heaven on my own merit."

You need help! You need blemish-less blood. You need a perfect sacrifice. You need a Savior. You need Jesus! Forget about your so-called friends and family for a minute. They are not going to be there to rescue you when you stand alone before the One who put this whole thing together, right? Don't fear man who after he has killed the body can do no more. Fear the One who after having killed the body can cast both the body and soul into hell. *"Fear Him!"* Jesus said.

Fear Him enough to recognize He's a holy God who rightly demands justice, yet still offers mercy and forgiveness to the ungodly. If you've lied once in your life, *you qualify!* You need a new heart and redemption, my precious soul.

Still not so sure you need a Savior? Let me help you out a little bit more because I'm your host on this tour of how you got to Heaven right? Right! So, check it out:

The 10 Commandments were never given by God for those living at the time or living now to *try to keep! Are you shocked and amazed? Many are! Why, though?*

Well, how can anyone know God, what He is like and what He commands without the Bible, his Word? But, oh! Even many people who are reading his Word are getting it wrong. The truth is important, my friend! One must rightly divide God's Word if one is to find salvation and live an abundant life here on earth, OK? Make sense? *Absolutely it does!*

You see, God has given the 10 Commandments to let guilty people know they are guilty. For example, if there were no speed limit signs, how could a traffic cop reasonably pull you over to write you a ticket? There was no law to transgress, right?

And so it is with the LORD God Almighty, Creator of Heaven and earth, Moral Law-Maker and Law-Giver and Judge over everybody. The Bible declares if you offend in just one part of the Law, you are guilty of it all. Care to have a glimpse at a few of the laws to see how you measure up? C'mon. Let's just peek at a few:

Thou shalt not lie. Have you ever lied in your life, even once? How many times? Take a guess. Hundreds? Thousands? Too much to count? Once? What would you call me if I lied to you? It rhymes with, "fire." Correct, you'd call me a, "liar." So, what are you? Correct. Please say the word out loud, to yourself. *"I am a _____."* Fill in the blank.

Great. Here's another one.

Thou shalt not take thy Lord's name in vain. Have you ever used God's name casually, or as a cuss word? Have you ever said, *"Oh my G—!"* This is taking the Lord's name in vain. It's called *blasphemy* when you do this. It's a very serious crime in God's eyes. He's the Judge, right? So, if I used God's name like this, what would you call me? A *blasphemer?* Right, so what are you? Say it out loud to yourself: *"I am a blasphemer."*

Thou shalt not steal. Have you ever taken anything which did not belong to you, irrespective of its value? A post-it pad from work? How about copyrighted papers or books? Music downloads? *Anything,* your entire life. If I stole something from you, what would you call me? A stealer? No. A *thief*, right? So, what are you? Are you a *thief?* Say it to yourself. If you ever took something which didn't belong to you—no matter when it was—how do you call it and more importantly, how does God call it? He gave the 10 Commandments, right?

Last one.

Jesus said if you look upon a woman with lust, you have committed adultery with that person in your heart, already. Have you ever in your life lusted after another person?

Knowing this definition from Jesus, if I admitted I had done this, what would you categorize me as? An *adulterer at heart?* Correct! So what are you? An *adulterer at heart?*

Now, we know Jesus claimed to be God in the flesh, right? So, God was having a visit to the earth, amongst His creation, and we gained further insight regarding how God defines His moral law. Isn't that correct?

Right! We just went through a few of those commandments and how did it go for you? There's no need for me to make a judgment of any sort upon you, right? You answered the questions to yourself, right?

Therefore, by your own admission and if you are honest with yourself, you probably came up with something like this: *"I am a lying, thieving, blaspheming, adulterer at heart." Close?*

Recognize my dear, precious soul ... these are only a few of the 10 Commandments. If God were to judge you by the 10 Commandments, how would you fare? *Innocent, or guilty? Heaven, or Hell?* Think for a moment. Think for two moments. I'll wait.

Are you concerned at all? I'm concerned *for you*, which is why I am here showing you how you got to Heaven. Much more refreshing than being condemned to Hell justly, isn't it? God is a good Judge!

Do you want justice, or *mercy?* I *know* you don't want the former, right? OK, then! *Let's move on and be all about this!*

So, as I was saying before the reality check: Fear Him enough to humble yourself and *cash in* on this new heart and all of the new covenant blessings being offered, OK? *Who is more worthy to be revered than the living God?*

Then and only then can you move past the *fear* of judgment and punishment. God would much rather you move into and onto love being perfected *within you*. Better? Good.

Remember. You cannot collect until you *pass Go*, though. *Who puts the cart before the horse?* You must surrender. You must lay down arms. You must stop rebelling against God via your lifestyle and your own opinions. Your opinions do not stand when in conflict with a perfect and holy God's Word, right? He's God, we are not, right? Good!

Instead of running away from God, you have decided to run towards God. You are deciding to trust Jesus because He has the pardon you need, right? What about that love though, too? Oh! *Amazing love!* Astonishing love. Dying for you, my friend. Dying for me. You know it. *Jesus!* He did it! *It's on! It's on!*

Refresher: We're here to get you home. You know this by now. Once you truly recognize your helpless condition before a holy God, then God can take you in your brokenness, put you back together and fill you with Himself; eternal Life. The road is *exclusive* in one sense and *inclusive* in another sense—as Jesus holds his arms wide open to all and says, *"Come! Whosoever shall call upon the name of the Lord shall be saved."*

Now, where are we on with this *weight* thing—you may be asking? Here's where we are. You're not going to do this half-heartedly. Nope. You are going to *go deep*. You approach your bed and you trust that thing to hold you, right? Some people *don't* have beds. If you have a bed, God has blessed you with a bed. Rejoice. Now, do you not look at this thing before you crash for the evening and say to yourself, ever:

"Ah ... this is good stuff. My feet hurt. My legs are weary. My back, oh ... my back. But it's all good now because in about two seconds, I'm going to get off these legs and put my full weight on this bed. Oh, hallelujah!"

Well, maybe you don't say it just like that—but work with me, here.

As your back cracks and your feet scream joyful praises up in your direction, you have now placed your full weight onto this bed of yours. You trusted this thing! You believed it would hold you. You didn't eyeball it and say, *"Hmm... will this thing hold me?* No! You had confidence and my friend, God *desires* and *expects* you to have confidence in Him, even *more so*.

"Come unto me, all you that labor and are heavy laden, and I will give you rest. Take my yoke upon you, and learn of me; for I am meek and lowly in heart: and you shall find rest unto your souls. For my yoke is easy, and my burden is light."
—Matthew 11:28-30 KJ2000

He knows this may not be easy at first, but He simply asks you to look at how much He loves you. He sent his one and only begotten Son on your behalf. This was so you would recognize his everlasting, passionate love for you! Look at the bloody cross where He expresses his love towards you. While you were *yet rebelling* against Him and his holiness by your actions *(lying, lusting, etc.)*, He laid it all down at the Cross—specifically for *you*. He knows the number of hairs on your head and He's really excited you're reading this book.

Why? It's because He has a lot more to say to you through his eternal Word, the Bible. *(God puts his Word above his name, which is Jesus. Jesus is the name above every name, so you know his Word is highly valued! Jesus is the Word. Jesus is the Word become flesh and dwelt among us.)*

For now though, we'll continue to *pour his eternal truth into you* throughout this book. *You need truth* in a world filled with lies. Just acknowledge amazing things are beginning to happen as you now have placed your full weight upon Him (Jesus) and Him alone!

By the way, since faith is analogous to trust, and according to God's offer—one can only be saved by grace through *faith*—which person really *trusts* Christ, or has *faith?* The person who *doesn't surrender their life into His care*, or the one who *does?*

C'mon, take a guess. Which one *trusts in Him?* Which one has genuine *faith* in Him? This is an easy one, right? The one who surrenders their heart and life into his care; am I right? Of course I'm right and of course you agree, because it's only logical!

This is why you have changed your mind about how much actual weight you must apply. It's because it makes complete sense to put your money where your mouth is by matching your lips up with your lifestyle and embracing what makes sense. You got to Heaven because instead of living a lie, you heard God's Spirit calling and you answered the call.

JESUS SPEAKS: "If you try to hang on to your life, you will lose it. But if you give up your life for my sake and for the sake of the Good News, you will save it."
—Mark 6:35 NLT

Oh? Not ready yet? *Of course you are!* We're getting you home to Heaven, are we not? So, let's do this. Keep your mind and heart open. God has plenty to show and pour into you. We're diving into it further right now, so hold on tightly!

About Righteousness. *"What's the big deal about righteousness?"* you might ask. *"As a matter of fact, what in the heck is it and why should I care?"* might be closer to the truth, if I were to guess?

Aha! It's OK. I hadn't always known about it or what it is, either. Why don't we do this? I'll give you the basics, but you at the same time, please cement this suggestion into your thinking: You will never want to let this term, never-ever want to let this term slip out of your vocabulary—once you recognize its significance, OK?

Very briefly, perhaps associate a shorter word and phrase with it, OK? *Righteousness* is to be declared *right* ... **with God.** Think of the term *justice* and its entire concept. Associate *just* with *right*. Righteousness is to be declared *just; just with God.*

So build upon it, briefly ... as it pertains to you. Since you have sinned *(e.g. lied, lusted, hated, etc.)* before a holy God and perfect, just Judge—you owe for the fine. The wage? Death. So, this is where Jesus comes in. Jesus didn't owe God's court anything, because He never committed any moral crimes or sins, right? Jesus is perfect, because Jesus is God in the flesh.

So again, where are you in this matter? Well, guilty, for one. How about Jesus? Innocent, right? Right. This is where righteousness comes in. Guilty people need a pardon, right? They need to be declared *just* or *right* or *righteous* before God. Else, the fine is pretty hefty. Death, eternal death. In other words, *Hell.*

We still have a problem, though. How do you get Christ's blemish-less record over to your account? This is a pretty big problem and gap, no? Absolutely! But you know what? Big problem, small God—yes?

But you see, your Creator isn't small, right? Of course not! God is *big!* God is *great!* That which is impossible with man is possible with God, right? Absolutely, my friend!

This is why even this huge, huge problem of: crimes, guilt, separation from God, wrath, judgment and Hell are *not too big for God.* God has made a way for you and we're here talking about it because we *gotta git* you home! Do we not? We *gotta git* you home and there's no time for playing games.

You are indeed reading this book and there are no coincidences. God is looking out for you. Let's go now! Forget about religion. Forget about all the nice things you've done. Forget about the bad things you've done, for now at least. Focus on what God has done in Jesus, because He's the One who is getting you home. He's the only One who *can!*

Imputation. *Imputed righteousness.* So again, how do you get Christ's blemish-less record over to your account? How do you become righteous in the eyes of God?

You become righteous the very moment you place that full weight upon Jesus to save you, as we discussed in the previous section. It's so easy, most people miss it. Even some professing Christians! Hey, tares grow with the wheat. Jesus will separate them in the end. The sheep from the goats. Don't be fooled by another Gospel. I'm giving you the Gospel of grace—the Gospel of Jesus Christ—in this book. Run from any other Gospel and do not underestimate what I am sharing with you. *Righteousness is key!*

Positionally, you need this righteousness to access eternal life. People are either righteous, thus *justified* before God on Judgment Day, or *not* righteous before a holy God on Judgment Day. In other words, if one is not made righteous by God, they are *condemned.*

However, this isn't you because God is opening your eyes as you read, right? *Right!*

So, to be *made righteous,* or to have God *impute righteousness (i.e. "credit" or "deposit" into your spiritual bank account from Christ's perfect account),* you need to trust Him with your life. If you don't surrender your life, it indicates you don't really trust Him to govern it; doesn't it follow? It reveals that you think you'd do a better job of it on your own, right? *Silliness!*

God is well able to govern His creation, is He not? Who aligned the sun to just the right distance from the earth so you wouldn't freeze or burn up from its rays? You know it! The list and examples go on and on. We don't have time for it all right now.

Seriously, though ... don't buy into the lie which caused you to be separated from God in the first place. Going to church or doing or not doing all sorts of other things—apart from this righteousness we're discussing—means *jack squat* in the grand scheme of things. I promise you. Let's major in the majors; not the minors. Shall we?

The Way of Righteousness. Therefore, to receive Him into your heart as Savior and recognize Him as Lord—*your* Lord—is to experience new birth. It's to be made righteous. It's all one package. There's only One, true God. There's only One, true Jesus. There's only One, true Way to eternal life, salvation and loving relationship with God the Father and his name is Jesus. *He* makes people righteous. This is why He came. This is why we have Christmas, Easter and acknowledge Him every time we date a check. This is God's plan and we're totally on it!

Are you with me? This is *turn-what-you-thought-was-right-side-up-living* into *upside-down-living-so-I-can-get-to-Heaven-living,* OK? There's no more important topic we could be discussing than right here and right now. Focus on what matters. Your eternity matters. God matters. Righteousness matters. Eternity is a long time. Unlike this brief and passing journey on this side of eternity, eternity never ends. You have to end up in the right place. Right places and right living come from right believing. Let's move towards finishing this thing out. *Ready?*

So, by submitting to Jesus as Lord, you openly confess Him to be so. His Word—the Holy Bible—instructs you as a blood-bought child of God. This is God's pathway to salvation. By grace alone, through faith alone, in Christ alone. Not the practicing of sacraments or some other un-biblical practice. Jesus isn't that complicated. He kicked it with the sinners that they might be transformed from sinners into sons; into daughters.

Rather than man's inventions, man's traditions, complicated doctrines influenced by Pagan religions and all other sorts of work-your-way-to-Heaven false teachings ... the One true and narrow path for you is: *by grace alone, through faith alone, in Christ alone.* This is what's going to get you home!

Trust me. You have God's Word on it, not some man-made tradition. Trust God and his Word. If He breathed out the stars, He's able to direct you to truth in his Word. We already covered this, right?

OK! So, hopefully this all helps you to get a better idea of what righteousness is and why it should matter to you.

Now, in order to change your mind about righteousness, you will need to let go of *detrimental* thinking. In other words—to get you home—you'll need to forsake or *abandon* some things.

Picture a hand squeezing something, then letting it go, completely. Or, picture in your mind's eye, a time when you *changed your mind*. A time when you *adjusted* or *corrected* your thinking. Perhaps you thought something such as your hairstyle or maybe a certain outfit looked cool on you. But, oh! You then looked back and said, *"What was I thinking!"* Pop culture said it was cool, but now you say, *"No way!"*

Only in *this current situation* of yours, following after popular beliefs and trends puts the destination of your very soul at stake! That's right! Which is why in this scenario, you will not look back and say, *"What was I thinking?"*

Instead, you will say, *"I'm glad that dude told me I must abandon certain things. Had I not listened and adjusted, those things were like cement blocks for shoes while water-skiing. Yikes!"*

So. How did you change your mind about righteousness?

Here's how:

You abandoned anything having to do with your own merit.

No longer do you think you can earn God's grace to merit Heaven. No longer, also, do you think faith is a small thing. God says even demons believe, and *shudder*.[vii] Demons won't be in Heaven. They were the angels who rebelled with Lucifer, now Satan. God has prepared another place for them.

Mere mental assent is a thing of the past for you because right now, God is showing you how you are saved. It's by the saving faith we have discussed.

At this moment, God the Holy Spirit supernaturally reveals an eternal truth of what is on the table, for you to consider:

> ***"For by grace you have been saved through faith. And this is not your own doing; it is the gift of God, not a result of works, so that no one may boast."***
> —Ephesians 2:8,9 ESV

Do you want this? It's available. God is speaking to His children. Do you want to be adopted as His child? Of course you do, because you want to not only go to Heaven but you want a meaningful love relationship with your real Papa, right? God is the Father of spirits. He sent his Son Jesus to save you. He calls people out from the crowd to follow Him. Special, unique children of God. People who strongly desire to take hold of what Jesus purchased for them at the Cross. I believe you want this. But how badly? Enough to make every single thing a distant second to Him?

This is the call. This is the call to faith. Is it you? I know it's you because we're in here chatting about it. What else is there? Those things the World offers which cannot save you on Judgment Day? Nonsense! In the reading of this book, God has reached out to you to pull you out of the pit! He's adjusting your thinking. He's wiping out errors with an eraser and moving you towards the Rock of his salvation—Jesus!

So on *righteousness*, you have recognized the need for a *change of mind regarding merit*. You have no merit apart from Christ. You have no Christ apart from faith. You are a new fan of righteousness because you like the way Christ deposits perfection into your account. Who wouldn't like it? *This is grace! Unmerited favor!* You don't earn it. You receive it! Here it is.

Do you want it? You have to abandon *self-righteousness*, or—leaning upon your own efforts. Are you willing to do it? If you are willing to do it, it will rock your world. It will change your life. It will change your view about God. It will explode into a whole new view of Jesus and what He has done for you. It will act as the foundation to your new and meaningful love relationship with your Heavenly Father. You will feel his warm embrace as you call Him, *"Papa."* And it's all because of Jesus you will do so.

Run *from* self-effort. Run *to* righteousness. God knew you couldn't merit it on your own, so abandon anything about your own merit. Run for your life from the temptation of pleading your own case as to why you deserve to go to Heaven! So many say they don't do this, but the tragedy is many do when we take a deeper look. They'll say, *"I trust what Jesus has done for me which is why I expect to go to Heaven. I'm not Hitler, after all!"*

Yet, when examined under the spotlight of truth and pressed to offer the reasons they plan to be accepted into God's Heaven, they'll say something like, *"Well, I'm a good person. I belong to such and such church, I take communion, I do this and I do that. You know, God is going to swing the door wide open for me! Yay!"*

My friend, run from this type of thinking! How do you get rid of it? Stop doing what you are doing and listening to what you are listening to. If it's your heart, ask Jesus for a new one because you need this, too, in order to get to Heaven. You get this when you follow and act upon what we have been discussing.

If it's a church, stop going to it. Find a new one. Find some good teaching and preaching. If you don't have a Bible, get one or read it, on-line. You can even listen to it, on-line. God's Word transforms your soul so however you *gots-to-git-it-in-you*, do it! Garbage in, garbage out. *(GIGO)*. How do you get a whole glass of orange juice from a half glass of water? *Keep pouring in the orange juice, right?*

So, I'll list some suggested, helpful resources for you at the end of the book. What you need is the pure truth of God's Word. You need Jesus. You need righteousness. You need to be *born-again*, according to Jesus. *(See or Google John 3:3)*

What else? You need to be adopted into God's family the way God has declared; not the way some church or tradition or religion declares *(if it conflicts with his Word)*. This is *your soul* and eternal destination we are discussing. God owns all souls, though and Christ has purchased yours at the Cross with his perfect, sinless blood. You have been bought at the highest price! You are of tremendous value to God. He proved it by becoming a Man and dying for you! Can you even believe it? Believe it! Stop pushing it to the side as if it's not such a big deal. *It is a big deal!* It's the biggest deal you will ever come across both here and forever. God wants to bring life ... *spiritual, eternal life* to your mortal body! Do you want it? Do you want Him?

Tomorrow isn't promised. Look. You or I can leave the house—just like my wife's former husband did one day—and never make it back home. Why? Because it was your scheduled last day on the earth. It happens every day. People physically die, then have to account for their lives, ultimately.

In this case, his name was Julio and he drove a big truck for a living. Enter stage left a female drunk driver. Julio never made it home as his truck burst into flames. God knew it was his last day on the earth, but just because He allowed it doesn't mean He caused it. God didn't get drunk this day—or any other day for that matter—and get behind some wheel intoxicated. No, sinful human beings going their own way are involved, are they not? Jesus also informs us there is a powerful, spiritual enemy of your soul prowling about.

What's my point? My point is: approximately *150,000 people die every, single day.* They were no doubt making plans for the coming days and weeks. What about eternity, though?

My friend, you do not know when your time will come! Either do I. Do not take this stuff for granted! You need a *new heart.* You need a *new mind.* You need a *new nature, the divine nature.*

You need *someOne else's merit*. You need a *Pardon*. God has all this for you waiting for you, already. His name is Jesus and He's knocking at the door of your heart and life. He wants in to seal you with His Spirit, but He isn't going to force His way in. You must invite Him into your heart. This is how you can have His merit, not your own. We read:

"I do not set aside the grace of God, for if righteousness could be gained through the law, Christ died for nothing!"
—Galatians 2:21

Christ died and rose for a reason. *YOU!* He knows the number of hairs on your head because He's amazing and He values you! Let God's Spirit permeate your entire being with all of these facts as they unfold before your very eyes. God is real, He loves you and He isn't talking just to kill time and to try to fit into your busy schedule. He's Ruler over all of creation, his name is Jesus and He wants and deserves preeminence in your life. He desires and deserves intimacy with you because all things were made by Him for Him. You were made to bring Him pleasure and He wants you to have pleasure in a relationship with Him. What a Creator and Savior!

Remember: God is Spirit. He became a Man to save you in the second Person of the Godhead, God the Son; Jesus Christ. He offers you his Holy Spirit, the Spirit of Christ, each proceeding from God the Father. God is One and He desires to be one in spirit with you! Interested? You're on your way to Heaven. Of course you are! This is getting good!

How else did you change your mind about righteousness?

You abandoned comparing yourself to others.

God has actually spoken on this matter, as well. Comparing ourselves with others is *not wise*.

All of your life, you have been taught to *measure yourself* against others. Performance, grades, looks, clothes, cars, jewelry, zip codes, area codes—you name it.

You have been given report cards and skills tests. Percentiles and so forth. How did you rate with the rest in comparison, for example? You are *contrasted* with colleagues. There's a lot of measuring going on and even necessary or beneficial in many situations. Others, not so much.

In all of this, you have been conditioned to measure yourself up to, down to and against other people. But look at this bit of truth:

" ... God sees not as man sees,

***for man looks at the outward
appearance, but the LORD looks at the
heart."***
—1 Samuel 16:7

When it comes to getting to Heaven, *getting you home* .... God isn't doing things the way the world system is doing things. Creator God never has quite done things the way the World does things. This is because He is Supreme and without Him, nothing would exist!

As it is, there is a *world system* and there is an enemy of your soul *looking to take you out* like a sniper on a top secret mission. A big problem for him though is ... God *is*. Right, God *is*. *God just is!*

This is a problem for the enemy of your soul. God is the great I AM. He just is! He always existed and always will exist. *He is!* Make sense?

Why is this important regarding this topic?

Quite simply, the fact God *is* means He is working in the midst of a world filled with deception. A world filled with lies where you are trying to get to Heaven, but somebody doesn't want you to get there. That's right!

In the spirit realm—the eternal realm which supersedes this flesh and blood physical realm—there's major conflict. You are at its center.

You see, hearts and minds—including yours and mine—come out of the gate *(i.e. the womb)* **blinded** to God's truth. This is all a result of *man's fall*—in the Garden. You recall this, right? The Garden of Eden?

Right. So, God warned Adam and Eve how to avoid certain tragedy. Did they refuse to listen to God? They probably hadn't planned to, but as can so often be the case ... *oh yeah!* It went down and this is why you are pretty much in a burning house with one way out. God is using me to flag you into the right direction! We know the outcome *(i.e. they partook of the fruit)*, so let's peek into the initial warning:

> *The LORD God took the man and put him in the Garden of Eden to work it and keep it. And the LORD God commanded the man, saying, "You may surely eat of every tree of the garden, but of the tree of the knowledge of good and evil you shall not eat, for in the day that you eat of it you shall surely die."*
> **—Genesis 15-17 ESV**

So, why do you need Jesus and what He offers *more* than you need church attendance, church membership, the same heart you started with, your own opinions and so forth? It brings me great joy to tell you why, because the words I speak to you are spirit and they are life.

It's because Jesus is the only One who solved your biggest problem: *separation from God.*

None of the aforementioned things—while perhaps not necessarily bad things—can solve your problem. Considering yourself better than the rapist on the evening news isn't going to get you home. If that dude finds righteousness by grace through faith in Jesus and you don't, how effective is your plan and your opinions? *Garbage*, right? *Useless* on that coming Great and Terrible Day, yes? God will judge the world in righteousness and the Father has given all authority to the Son. Jesus has been appointed the ultimate Judge. Did you know this? It's true.

You see, Jesus didn't come to judge the first time. You are still in this window of *grace*. We are capitalizing upon this currently open window in order to get you home. Why? It's because *Jesus came to save.*

This opportunity is now for *you!* Once this window of time closes, Jesus is scheduled to *come back* to judge the living and the dead. His Kingdom will have no end. Amen?

Exactly. So, is it worth comparing yourself to others, or is this one worth throwing away, too? *Exactamundo! Trash it.* You don't need or want this one any longer, my friend. Kiss it, *"Goodbye!" Arrivederce, Larry! So long and sayonara to "people-comparing"*—right?

Still not convinced? Again, trust me. Trust Jesus. Trust God's eternal Word—the Bible. It declares it. You cannot stand on your own before a holy, perfect God. He isn't extending *Heaven invitations* by grading you as *compared to other people*. This is the wrong plan if it's the one to which you are holding. *Abandon ship!*

Comparing yourself with others is a death-trap, just like so many other things in this world. If you want to stand on your own, God must then compare you to His perfect, blemish-less, Lamb-of-a-Son: Jesus Christ. Are you sure you want to put your record up against His?

Suicide! Don't even think about it! God is only going to be interested in one question: *"What did you do with my Son, Jesus?"*

Therefore, one more time: *Stop comparing.* You will lose either way because you can't meet God's standard of righteousness on your own. God must impute it to you as a gift. There's no other way. So, since there's no other way—abandon the daily, self-righteous comparisons and *get on board with the Savior, Jesus!* Clothe yourself in *His* righteousness!

Can you see now why people are self-proclaimed Jesus freaks? It's because God has helped them to understand something. That something is *to know* that—apart from inviting Jesus in to live his life through them via faith—there *is no righteousness*.

That's right. The case has been tried and there has been rendered a verdict. *Guilty!* Eternity in Hell because God is a *good* Judge. His name is Jesus and He's punishing all evil-doers, down to the smallest of breeches. He is *infinitely holy* and He therefore must punish crime. What good Judge let's rapists run free? Yet, to speak *even one lie* is a crime punishable by death in a holy God's courtroom.

This is why He punished His Son on the Cross. Do you want the Pardon this precious blood at the Cross offers? Or, are you going with another plan? There is no other plan, my friend.

I know what you are doing because this is about you got to Heaven, right? You are abandoning your own merit and comparing yourself with others. Rather than compare yourself to others or to Jesus, you are choosing instead to *receive* Jesus along with His *imputed righteousness!* Can a brotha get an, *"Amen?" You know it's going down because* **you are going up!**

As a child of God and on behalf of my born-again brothers and sisters in Jesus, let me ask you to please marinate in these following two verses. Let God transform your soul as faith comes by hearing and hearing ... by the Word of Christ:

> **"Therefore, we are ambassadors for Christ, as though God were making an appeal through us; <u>we beg you on behalf of Christ, be reconciled to God. He made Him who knew no sin to be sin on our behalf, so that we might become the righteousness of God in Him."</u>**
> —**2 Corinthians 5:20, 21 NASB**

This is the basis of the *imputed righteousness* we've been discussing throughout this extended section. This is how God set you up for this *trust option* now being presented before you. God must legally make a way to transfer perfection into an imperfect account if a Pardon is to be offered.

Your path is now narrow because God is opening your eyes to the seriousness of this gift of righteousness and also of your *getting it right*. It's not to be taken lightly. Grasping and embracing this is what is going to get you home; *I'm tellin' ya!*

Huge chunks of society are walking right past this supernatural transaction offer. This *was you* but today is a new day! No more getting this one wrong! Otherwise, you'd be in that tragic *poser* category—having gone the way of Cain and those who did it, *"My way."*

Don't do it *your way*. Do it *God's way*. Jesus is *The Way*. He's the Giver of Life. He designed every strand of DNA and created all living things. Yeah! His name is Jesus and there is no name above His Name.

One day soon, *every knee will bow and every tongue will confess* Jesus Christ is Lord to the glory of God the Father. *He created you* that He'd have a home in your heart. You are to never be alone, again. *Posers* walk and talk and claim to be carrying the Holy Spirit as they stand right next to genuine believers.

However, God knows who is sealed with his Spirit when they invite Christ in—and He knows who is not. *Just say no* to the *weed* and instead, get on board by being you *some of that wheat!*

"Let both grow together until the harvest. At that time I will tell the harvesters: 'First collect the weeds and tie them in bundles to be burned; then gather the wheat and bring it into my barn.'"
—Matthew 13:30 NIV

Don't forget. <u>He who knew no sin</u> *became sin for you, and for me.* This is very sobering, isn't it? Consider what is on the table and what can *possibly* be credited to your spiritual bank account. *Jesus overpaid for you!*

In other words, have you ever left a generous tip while out to eat, perhaps? *Yeah, Jesus left a serious tip on your behalf! (You can learn more about those critical details in the other Bible Insights Collection books.)*

Recognize: *Jesus has you covered.* Nevertheless, you must respond to his finished work @Calvary by accepting Him into your heart. You must do this *by grace through faith* in order for the imputation to occur. Then and only then can your account be justly credited. No longer will your account be in the red. Instead, it will overflow with plenty of Christ's sinless blood to shield you on that coming *Great and Terrible Day!*

About Certainty. How do you change your mind about being certain? Choose against being uncertain. You see, the first thing God wants you to do is be certain about his finished work on the Cross—in the Person of God the Son. We talked about placing your full weight upon what He has done in a previous section, right?

So now, you need to realize and seal it into your mind God is serious about you being *seriously certain*. Certain about salvation. Certain you are going to Heaven, and only based upon taking the narrow path He has laid out. Yes? Not your way. This isn't McDonald's. This is the way out of a house on fire. We're not eating a big breakfast, here. Your entire existence is on fire and we're learning how you let God put it out and take you home, remember?

Yeah! So, your zeal, your confidence needs to be based upon truth; not speculation. Not pop culture, either. *"Oh, God is forgiving so yeah, yeah, well I'm OK because God forgives everybody and it'll all work itself out. It's all good in the hood."*

No my friend! It's *not all good in the hood* for a mentality like the above. And, it's only going to get worse for the person who doesn't stop in their tracks of life and start majoring in the majors. People under grace *do not have sin as their master*. They have Jesus and righteousness—and, they know it!

> **_"I write these things to you who believe in the name of the Son of God so that you may <u>know</u> that you have eternal life."_**
> —1 John 5:13

They not only know it, but their lives reflect this change. Trust me, when you go from being dead in your sins to being alive in Christ, there's going to be a recognizable change. In one existence, you lived for yourself, orphaned. Scared to die.

In this new life and existence, God is your Daddy *for real*. You also begin to live for Jesus as God takes up residence in your heart. He gives eternal life to your mortal body and you are never the same because you actually have trusted Jesus. *What a Savior!*

You'll never be unsure about Heaven because your faith will be in the right place. Not in your church, not in your filthy rags of self-righteousness and not in some other message.

Rather, you will have certainty because your faith and full weight in Jesus has taken God at his Word and God cannot lie. So, you're anchored for good. Seriously good stuff right there, yeah? Yes!

"But what things were gain to me, those I counted loss for Christ. Yea doubtless, and I count all things but loss for the excellency of the knowledge of Christ Jesus my Lord: for whom I have suffered the loss of all things, and do count them but dung, that I may win Christ, And be found in him, <u>not having mine own righteousness</u>, which is of the law, but that <u>which is through the faith of Christ, the righteousness which is of God by faith:</u>"
—Philippians 3:7-9 KJV

You will learn it is Christ's obedience, Christ's faith and Christ's death and resurrection on your behalf which not only saves you, but continues to save you as you get going on your way to Heaven. God is giving you faith—right now—to let it all ride on Jesus and continue to ride on Jesus. Why? So you can have fire insurance and avoid Him?

Let it never be! No way! He's done all of this because He loves you and desires to walk with you and live in and through you. Now, that's intimacy! *In-to-me-see,* right? Yeah, right! God will make your mind and life *explode* with joy. I'm telling you, He will give you a peace that surpasses understanding. *It's real, yo!*

"O taste and see that the LORD is good; How blessed is the man who takes refuge in Him!"
—Psalm 34:8 NASB

Jesus said the following regarding eternal life:

> **"Whoever loves his life loses it, and whoever hates his life in this world will keep it for eternal life."**
> —John 12:25

Many might say, *"This is a hard teaching. Who can make sense of it?"*

My friend, *you* will make sense of it because it's central to this journey! The payment to cover your multitude of sins was a hard road for Jesus, too. He sweat great drops of blood prior to heading off to be *beaten to a bloody pulp* on that brutal road to the Cross. He did this for you. He did this because God so loved *you* ... He sent his only Son to die in *your* place for *your* sins. *Mine, too!*

Should this move you? It does move you because you are one of those who are on your way to Heaven. So ...

How did you get to Heaven? You changed your mind ...

About Selfish Ambition. Right! You trusted in Him as your LORD, which translated effectively to you *hating your life,* in turn— saving it. Having those ears to hear, God revealed to you since it's not about you but what Jesus has done on the Cross *for you, you embraced his direction. His direction*—as much as it didn't seem to make sense—is for you to no longer live for yourself. Rather, it's to live for Him and Him, alone. In doing so, you both *save* and *find* your life!

"The acts of the flesh are obvious: sexual immorality, impurity and debauchery; idolatry and witchcraft; hatred, discord, jealousy, fits of rage, <u>selfish ambition</u>, dissensions, factions and envy; drunkenness, orgies, and the like. I warn you, as I did before, that those who live like this will not inherit the kingdom of God."
—Galatians 5:19-21 NIV

Jesus has proven Himself to be the Author of Life. This is why those who experienced Him were persuaded of who He was/is.

"... and you killed the Author of life, whom God raised from the dead. To this we are witnesses."
—Acts 3:15

While we're on the topic of those who experienced Him being persuaded of He was and is, let's not forget how Christianity began. Unlike the terrorists who flew jet planes into the twin towers, Christ's followers were claiming they saw Jesus raised from the dead.

The terrorists died for what they thought was true *(e.g. that they were doing right, according to truth, and would be heading into the arms of awaiting virgins.)*

On the other hand, Christ's followers also believed they were dying for the truth. Two very different pictures of truth, though. What's more, consider the further contrast and where it leads:

The terrorists died for what they thought to be true. Even though many would disagree with this being the truth, these men still went into the whole thing believing their actions were true and the appropriate path to Heaven.

So, one could logically conclude they died for what they believed to be true, right? Right.

Now, consider Christ's followers. Do you know why all were put to death in horrific fashions, save one? It's because each of them experienced Jesus before the crucifixion, then either saw him or knew him to be crucified on that Cross of Calvary.

Yet, here's the kicker. All who were put to death were put to death because they would not recant on *seeing* the *risen* Christ. Yeah! They died for what they <u>believed to be true</u>, as well! Right?

Therefore, it follows that: these men *would have had to have known they were dying for a lie* had they actually *not seen* Jesus alive again—from the dead. This wouldn't make any sense, though!

Who *knowingly* dies for a lie? *Exactly!* This is why it's helpful for you to know and remember how this whole salvation movement began: with an *empty tomb!*

So when we talk about this *Author of Life*, it's critical we attribute credit where credit is due. This is amazing news for you! If anyone knows how one is to *actually locate* and *live* this thing called, *"Life,"* let's all agree: *It would be Jesus!* Jesus is the Author of Life!

Hence, we need to *"lean in"* and pay attention to what He is saying, right? Yes, correct! And Jesus ... what is one of the things You can offer regarding this salvation topic? How can this precious soul know how they actually got to Heaven?

> ***JESUS SPEAKS:*** ***"If you try to hang on to your life, you will lose it. But if you give up your life for my sake and for the sake of the Good News, you will save it."***
> —Mark 8:35 NLT

Whoa! So you see my friend? It's *upside-down* thinking in order to get things *right-side* up. The Author of Life has spoken. Jesus is pointing you into the right direction. *You knew it was on* and the *way to* and the *truth about* Heaven continues to be revealed.

Amazing grace, how sweet the sound! Jesus confirms you got to Heaven, *how?* By letting go of your life, in the sense you now *trust* Him to govern it. *Faith baby, faith! Faith in Christ. (OK, you're not my baby—so just work with me, here!)*

How does Jesus govern you, as Lord over all of Creation? Why, by His Spirit and His Word, of course. Jesus speaks to you today both spirit ... and life.

"Choose life," He cries. *"Whoever is thirsty, let them drink freely from the fountain of Life!"* Jesus says, *"I AM the Life! Come unto Me. Trust in Me. Trust in my Word."*

Do you trust Him? Who is more trustworthy than Jesus? *Now we're getting somewhere!*

You changed your mind about making excuses.

You didn't just change your mind about making excuses, you changed your mind about making *lame* excuses.

When it comes to pushing away the things which *don't matter* and embracing the only One *who* matters, multitudes today get it wrong. They might be *leaning in*, but they are leaning into the wrong people or things. There's only *One* thing to lean into and the *it* is a *He* and the *He* is *Jesus Christ*.

Make no mistake about it. You got to Heaven because you changed your mind about the excuses. You dropped the sum of *zero* and instead—got with the *Hero!*

Jesus knew people would do this, so He put forth an example of just how *lame* the lame excuses really sound. We read:

> ***Jesus replied with this story: "A man prepared a great feast and sent out many invitations. When the banquet was ready, he sent his servant to tell the guests, 'Come, the banquet is ready.' But they all began making excuses. One said, 'I have just bought a field and must inspect it. Please excuse me.'"***
> —Luke 14:16-18 NLT

Who buys a field without first inspecting it? *Lame!*

So you can see, excuses which are being made by the masses today about Jesus ... whether they are playing church membership or openly rejecting Him, are in the same condition. They are lost and without a saving, loving, meaningful relationship with God, through Jesus—God the Son. They are filled with excuses.

"I attend church. Stop Bible-thumping. What has gotten into you?"

The Holy Spirit has gotten into me because I invited Him in to save me! That's what has gotten into me. It's an open invitation to the banquet but most people have lame excuses, as if any excuse is good enough!

Are you not done with excuses, friend? Of course you are done with them! Why in the world would you investigate this book, otherwise? Wise men and women still seek Him. Are you a seeker? *Yes! You are!* This is what you want to be! Seek God! *He's not lost, but you have been.*

Let's further solidify this. You need God because the facts of the matter are He created you to walk with Him. His desire is to enjoy you and you, Him. He promises to guide and comfort you until you see Him face-to-face. There's coming that one, magnificent and glorious day for those who trust Him. You are going to let Jesus take you home because you aren't going to that *other place*, am I right? Back me up!

"And without faith it is impossible to please Him, for he who comes to God must believe that He is and that He is a rewarder of those who seek Him."
—Hebrews 11:6

Summary

You've learned a lot in this chapter. It's been a huge chapter. We've covered much and as you can see, the simplest thing can oftentimes end up being the most difficult thing, right?

Nevertheless, it need not remain the case! What are we talking, here? Correct. Simply changing your mind. Wisdom dictates one changes their mind and opinion about a thing when it's makes good sense to do so.

Remember. We're not just talking about changing your mind about whether or not God exists. That is the obvious part. God has made his existence clear, even without the Gospel of Jesus:

> *"For since the creation of the world God's invisible qualities--his eternal power and divine nature--have been clearly seen, being understood from what has been made, so that people are without excuse."*
> —Romans 1:20

Rather, God has just revealed in a very powerful way—specifically to and for you—that you must change your mind:

1) About his Word, the Bible
2) About who Jesus is
3) About how much weight you must apply
4) About certainty
5) About selfish ambition

6) About letting go of your life
7) About making lame excuses

Life Application

1. What have you thought in the past about God's Word, the Holy Bible? Have you formed a different opinion about it, now?

2. Who do you say Jesus is?

3. Are you able to stand before God on Judgment Day on your own merit? If so or if not, why?

4. Are your goals and aspirations apart from Christ's good news worth pursuing as a bigger priority? Why do you believe this?

5. Will any of your past or current excuses aid you in getting to Heaven? Will you keep them or release them? Which is the wiser option and why?

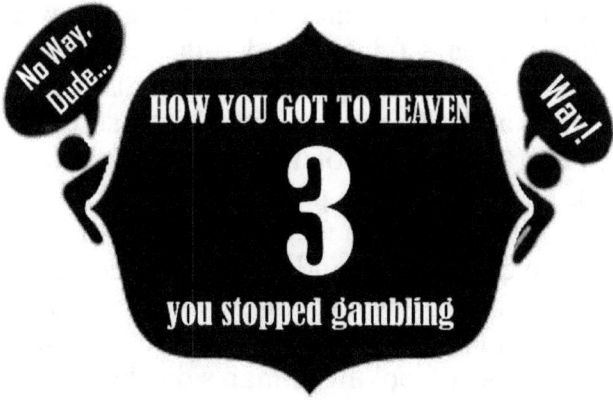

How Did You Get To Heaven?
YOU STOPPED GAMBLING
With Your Soul

As the Creator, God actually owns *all* souls.[viii]
Nevertheless, you as a *spirit* possess a soul and a body. The last thing you want to do is gamble with your soul. Your soul is eternal and desperately requires atonement in order to be cleansed from all sin and have relationship with God. Relationship with God and Heaven are infinitely connected. You cannot have one without the other, OK?

Additionally, you should also be made aware of the fact that God is a good Judge. He has revealed to each of us His system of justice requires a blood sacrifice. Since sin is so wicked and nasty in the eyes of a loving, holy and just God, He must require payment for it. It all started in the Garden when blood was shed in order to cover Adam and Eve. It replaced their own attempt to cover themselves (i.e. fig leaves) and took place after their disobedience. What's another way of looking at man's disobedience? It's a *lack of trusting in and obeying God's Word.*

As time moved along, God revealed further the requirement for this blood, which was a shadow of things to come—Christ's shed blood on the Cross. We read:

> **"For the life of a creature is in the blood, and I have given it to you to make atonement for yourselves on the altar; it is the blood that makes atonement for one's life."**
> —Leviticus 17:11 NIV

###

> **"In fact, the law requires that nearly everything be cleansed with blood, and without the shedding of blood there is no forgiveness."**
> —Hebrews 9:22 NIV

Therefore, and with this in mind, let's further discover how you got to Heaven. All contents of this book are critical to your understanding and these next points are no exception.

Now, what are some key indicators pertaining to a proper outlook as it relates to the care of your soul? It's clear. You will discontinue anything remotely suggesting you are gambling with your soul. You want Heaven to be true and not false for you, right? *Right!*

So, how do you know you have stopped gambling with your soul?

Here's how. It is:

Because you counted the cost. God didn't spare His best *(i.e. one and only Son)* to rescue you from your sins. Nor is He holding back any good thing from you. As you begin to tally up the incredible promises He has made and guaranteed to those who love Him, you can begin to see why God *is* love.

In other words, God is *all in* when it comes to having a meaningful, eternal relationship with *you*. Aren't you tired of placing your trust in the things of this world which always over-promise, yet never fully satisfy? *Of course you are!* God has better and because He knows better, He's calling on you to go all in, as well.

How does He advise you to approach this relationship? We read:

"But don't begin until you count the cost. For who would begin construction of a building without first calculating the cost to see if there is enough money to finish it?"
—Luke 14:28 NLT

DUDE-CAM
JESUS
KING of KINGS
"I'm
ALL IN..."
"No Way,
Dude!"
"Dude,
No Way!"
Life
.eternity
FOREVER IS A LONG TIME. PLAY WISELY.
ChristFollowers

That's right! In Jesus, God has expressed *agape* love to you. True, eternal love. It's that sacrificial love, the love of God. It's not the counterfeited love—which is *selfish* love. Who needs another selfish person? You need God's Spirit! Every person needs God's Spirit because a person without God is dead. Spiritual bankruptcy is death! You need life if you're going to make it home and experience bliss forever and ever.

> **"Blessed are the poor in spirit, for theirs is the kingdom of heaven."**
> —Matthew 5:3 NIV

The sooner you can admit you are spiritually bankrupt apart from a surrendered life to Jesus, the sooner you can be made whole. The sooner, also, you can start enjoying the abundant life He offers in this relationship. Count the cost. The gift is free, but it cost God a tremendous price: *his One and only Son. God the Son!* Jesus Christ. God in the flesh.

Because you didn't fear man. Dear friend, God is omniscient *(= all-knowing)*, He is omnipresent *(= all-present)* and He is omnipotent *(= all-powerful)*. If we should have concern regarding what anyone thinks, let's stop majoring in the minors, shall we?

Now, we touched upon this earlier. However, let's go ahead and solidify it with the reference verse from God's eternal Word. Ready? Here we go:

> *JESUS SPEAKS: "I say to you, My friends, do not be afraid of those who kill the body and after that have no more that they can do. But I will warn you whom to fear: fear the One who, after He has killed, has authority to cast into hell; yes, I tell you, fear Him! Are not five sparrows sold for two cents? Yet not one of them is forgotten before God. Indeed, the very hairs of your head are all numbered. Do not fear; you are more valuable than many sparrows."*
> —Luke 12

As you marinate in this verse, have you noticed how Jesus is directing you towards who appropriately is worthy to be revered and with whom you ought to be concerned? I know you did! It isn't other people, is it? Absolutely not!

Conversely, isn't Jesus so beautiful in His balance of grace and truth? This is how He came to us—in grace and truth. *Filled* with grace and truth!

So on one hand and in one sense, Jesus is instructing us as to not fear man but rather, have an appropriate fear of God. On the other hand and in another sense *(which then necessarily cancels out any chance of contradiction),* Jesus expresses how valuable you are to your Creator, who desires to be your Heavenly Father—*by adoption.*

This is right at the door because *Jesus is now at the door of your heart,* knocking. *(We'll look again at this, shortly.)* For now, understand the only one on this planet you should be concerned with *is God.* Major in the *majors.* Don't major in the *minors.* You plus God equals the majority in every, single situation. The way to have God on your side is to be in Christ. You want your life to be hidden in Christ and this is where you are headed.

"He will cover you with his feathers, and under his wings you will find refuge; his faithfulness will be your shield and rampart."
—Psalm 91:4 NIV

"Therefore, if anyone is in Christ, the new creation has come: The old has gone, the new is here!"

—2 Corinthians 5:17

Summary

In highlighting this chapter for a brief review, you came to learn or at least re-affirm some foundational truths regarding how you got to Heaven—as it relates to your soul.

God has revealed to you there is a payment for sin and *since sin's payment is death,* innocent blood must be shed. This is required of God to provide payment for the crime. The animal or animals God sacrificed to cover Adam and Eve—after their lack of trust in Him and his Word—reveals others are impacted when we sin. Sin always brings forth death; *always.* Again, we read:

> ***"Let no man say when he is tempted, I am tempted of God: for God cannot be tempted with evil, neither tempts he any man: But every man is tempted, when he is drawn away of his own lust, and enticed. Then when lust has conceived, it brings forth sin: <u>and sin, when it is finished, brings forth death.</u>"***
> **—James 1:13-15 KJ2000**

Therefore, you've discovered sin is no small matter. It put Jesus on the Cross—in your place *and* in my place. The current deal is, I'm here to guide you on how to cash in at Christ's expense. He didn't pay this high price so the *payment* and *pardon* would go unclaimed, right? God has a purpose for what He does and His greatest desire is to have you take hold of all He is offering, in Jesus.

Remember: When the call came for Jesus to take on flesh and carry out this rescue mission on your behalf, He didn't decline. He willingly raised His hand and willingly carried that old, rugged Cross after having already been beaten and bloodied beyond recognition. They spat in his face!

Yet, when He thought of you, He counted His own cost and decided to *lay it all down:*

> **<u>"Because of the joy awaiting him, he endured the cross, disregarding its shame</u>. Now he is seated in the place of honor beside God's throne."**
> —Hebrews 12:2 NLT

As you may have surmised, Jesus isn't interested in half-hearted relationships. Are you? Have you settled for less? Whether you have or not—I think if you're honest with yourself—you'd agree a passionate, loving relationship is where *it's at*. Am I right?

Hey, if you've lost that loving feeling, it's time to get connected to the Savior, OK? Even if you haven't lost that loving feeling, nobody's going to out-do Jesus when it comes to love. Jesus is love and He desires relationship *with you.*

Stop fearing man and other people around you. Dig into a relationship with the *Giver of Life* and let *Him* show you how to love. He wants to live His life through you so you can experience a love and life which is *everlasting.*

Do you want it? How can you not want it? It's readily available and we're gonna do coffee or orange juice or something good in Heaven, so get on this *J-Train, yo!*

We're almost through talkin'—so what are we gonna do, now? You know what we're gonna do. *Let's gooooo!* Only a few more tiny chapters remaining.

Life Application

1. Have you been gambling with your soul? If so, what are the changes you will make to change this reality?

"For what shall it profit a man, if he shall gain the whole world, and lose his own soul?"
—Mark 8:36 KJV

"What good is it for someone to gain the whole world, yet forfeit their soul?"
—Mark 8:36 NIV

2. Is putting a halt to this type of gambling worth it? Why or why not?

3. Who owns your soul? If you possess this soul, have you taken the necessary steps for its atonement?

God's Purpose

God's purpose is for man to serve, honor and walk with Him. What then, is man's issue!

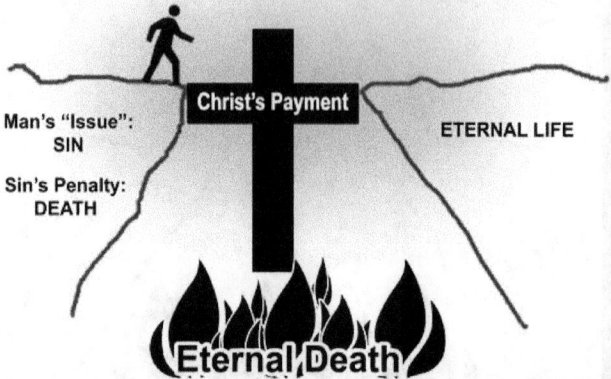

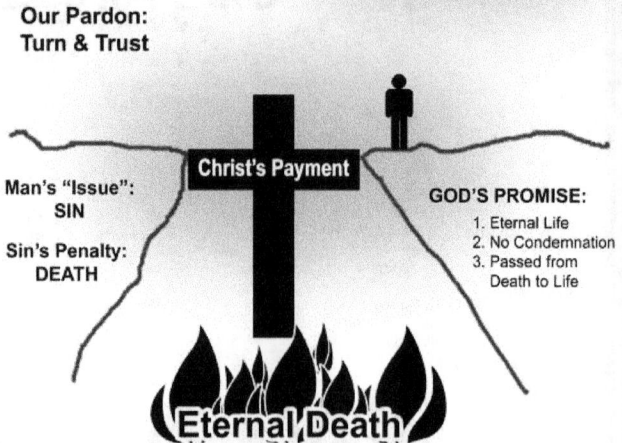

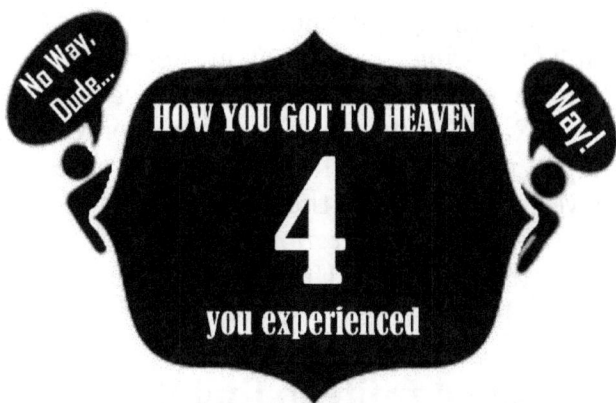

HOW YOU GOT TO HEAVEN

4

you experienced

How Did You Get To Heaven?
YOU EXPERIENCED

A Conversion

This is why Matthew 18:3 was cited way back at the start of this book. Here we are again. This is not a small matter. According to your Creator, you *must have a conversion in order to get to Heaven*. God expects you to stop playing adult when it comes to how you handle the whole forgiveness and Heaven offer. There's a time after conversion to begin your growth and leave childish things behind.

For now though, it's not before you *pass Go—which is* inviting Jesus into your heart to rule and to reign. This is the *Go part*, so *we gotsta go, yo! Right? C'mon.* We're almost home. We're going to now dig into the meat and potatoes of Heaven. This is where the rubber meets the road, as it were. *Let's keep it moving!*

How did you get to Heaven by way of conversion?

You lost your life to find it. You chose to live by faith. Long before Jesus came, God was calling people into Heaven and it has always been by *faith.* Faith in what or who? It's been *faith in God* which has *always centered upon the finished work of Jesus Christ.*

Correct! People in the *B.C.* timeframe of the calendar trusted God by faith. They did so in looking *ahead* to God sending Jesus. Just as we look *back* to Christ's finished work as the perfect offering for our crimes against God, those folks looked ahead.

So, what does this have to do with losing your life to find it? Plenty! How much *faith,* or more specifically—how much *faith in Christ* does it take to hold onto your life and attempt to direct it by yourself? I'm waiting. Correct. None!

On the other hand, does it require *faith* in Jesus to instead *surrender your life to Him* and *live under His direction and Lordship?* Absolutely! Look. There are many *religious* posers out there. Don't be one of them! There won't be any posers in Heaven, so since you're going to Heaven, *just say no to po-po!* OK? If you've been posing, no more posing. This stuff is *for real, yo!*

"For whoever wishes to save his life will lose it; but whoever <u>loses</u> his life for My sake will <u>find</u> it."
—Matthew 16:25

###

"Behold, as for the proud one, His soul is not right within him; But the <u>righteous will live by his faith.</u>"
—Habakkuk 2:4 NASB

###

"Look at the proud! They trust in themselves, and <u>their lives are crooked</u>. But the <u>righteous</u> <u>will live by their faithfulness to God.</u>"
—Habakkuk 2:4 NASB

###

"Behold, his soul which is lifted up is not upright in him: but <u>the just shall live by his faith</u>."
—Habakkuk 2:4 KJV

# # #

For in the gospel the righteousness of God is revealed--a righteousness that is by faith from first to last, just as it is written: "<u>The righteous will live by faith.</u>"
—Romans 1:17 NIV

# # #

And, "But <u>my righteous one will live by faith</u>. And I take no pleasure in the one who shrinks back."
—Hebrews 10:38 NIV

# # #

Clearly <u>no one who relies on the law is justified before God</u>, because "the <u>righteous will live by faith</u>."
—Galatians 3:11 NIV

Is God making an effort to show how those on their way to Heaven live? I'd say so! Wouldn't you? Also, what is *"living by the law?"* Why, lacking *surrender* to Jesus. When you choose to not surrender in faith to Jesus and His Lordship, you are saying to God: *"I got this one on my own, God. I don't need to surrender to Jesus. I know what Jesus did, but I'm getting into Heaven because of what I've done and am doing as I try to appease you with my <u>righteous deeds</u>, OK?"*

This is trying to live by *law*, not by *grace* through *faith*. Living by the law leaves you guilty before God because you can't do it, can you? Of course you can't. God is holy. Let's see what God says about attempting to present your so-called *righteous deeds* before Him as opposed to living a *surrendered life of faith in Jesus*. We read:

"We are all infected and impure with sin. When we display <u>our righteous deeds</u>, they are nothing but filthy rags. Like autumn leaves, we wither and fall, and our sins sweep us away like the wind."
—Isaiah 64:6 NLT

Are you familiar with what a female menstrual rag is? Unpleasant thought, isn't it? Yet, when a person decides to go outside of God's narrow plan of redemption, this is the picture we are left with, from God.

God is basically saying, as I use my own DNA to describe it—*"I have given you my One and only Son, Jesus. I placed Him onto the Cross so you would hopefully place your full trust in Him as the only sacrifice which would satisfy My holy standard of righteousness, through faith. Instead, you are rejecting My plan and attempting to bring me a big pile of menstrual rags, expecting Me to be happy with your offering. Is this what you are doing? Seriously?"*

So, you really don't want to go this route which is why God places this book and me into your path. He wants you in Heaven with Him and you plan to go to Heaven too, right? Yeah! So, this is all necessary to make sure the lies of this world aren't going to continue to hold you captive, right? Yes! It appears to all have been necessary.

Do you want God to grab Christ's perfect record of the blameless, sinless life He lived and use it when He's deciding upon your fate this coming Judgment Day?

"Come now, let us settle the matter," says the LORD. "Though your sins are like scarlet, they shall be as white as snow; though they are red as crimson, they shall be like wool."
—Isaiah 1:18 NIV

Wow. An answer to your biggest issue. How to be made right with God. To think God is using his Word to reason with you and present such an offer to you. You can now see why faith becomes central to this whole thing. Faith in Christ because Jesus solves your problem. You can only bring filthy menstrual rags to God via your righteous deeds, right? We just read it. Faith in the finished work of Jesus, however, delivers that imputed righteousness to your account. Right? *Right, again!*

So once more, how does one become *just,* or *righteous?* We covered this earlier, remember? You abandoned every single ounce of your own merit and instead placed your *full weight on* and *trust in … Christ's finished work at the Cross,* right? No resumes. No bragging on all of your charitable causes and church attendance records, right?

Only confidence in what Jesus has done, which will turn your world upside down which is actually then right-side up. Agreed? Good! *The just shall live by faith.* The *righteous shall live by faith in Jesus Christ.* You will act differently. You will speak differently. Instead of being under your own direction, you will be sealed with and filled with God's Holy Spirit by grace *through faith,* right?

Yes! Jackpot! Never forget this simple phrase, then. The *just* shall *live* by *faith!* Only those God declares just or righteous end up in Heaven. This is why you will now live *by faith alone in Christ alone. Can I get an Amen all up in here? Man, this is good!* God is pouring His eternal truth out and directly into you, right now. Tell Him you're ready. Tell Him you're ready. Do you know how long He's been waiting for you? God is crazy about you! *C'mon now!*

Faith's cost. Anything worth *anything* has a cost, right? *"There's no free lunch!"* many will say. Do you think anyone needs to inform Jesus about this? Me neither.

To be sure, God's grace is free. It's available to everyone. Faith does seem, however, to carry along with it a cost. Jesus said we need to count the cost, right?

Right! Count the cost of leaving behind your shame, guilt and condemnation. Count the cost of being associated with the One who bled and died for you. Yeah, count the cost. Count how many heartaches you will now avoid as you place your full weight on the only sure and solid thing this life has to offer. Understand all who desire to live godly in Christ Jesus shall be persecuted.[ix] People will hate you because they hated Jesus, first. Go ahead, count the cost. Hell canceled. Ouch, what a horrible cost to follow Jesus. You don't get to go into eternal, conscious torment. What a loss there. Oh man, eternal bliss. Man, *horrible,* right?

> *"You make known to me the path of life; in your presence there is <u>fullness of joy</u>; <u>at your right hand are pleasures forevermore</u>."*
> —Psalm 16:11 ESV

So, prepare. There is a cost. It's also critical for you to realize many, many people have Christianity wrong. Many are looking in from the outside drawing the wrong conclusions. They haven't humbled themselves to receive Christ, nor to then allow God to open their blinded minds to the revelation of his Word. Something else always seems to be more interesting than what God has to say. God is speaking, though. He has a lot to share with you about the ways in which He calls you to live this thing out.

Why is this important? You're in the right hands, my friend. I told you we are going to get you home by you discovering just how you got there.

It's important because as God commonly does, you are getting a glimpse of things beforehand as I use God's Word to reveal eternal truth to you. God tells the end from the beginning because He's God. He is also quite happy to share this unique insight with you, as you *lean in*. This is the only type of *leaning in* God wants you to do before you *lean into* anything else, OK? It's all about Jesus. Lean into God by leaning into Jesus.

By the way, before we examine this idea, do you know the angels *lean in* when it comes to those who have faith in Christ? Yeah! They are *leaning in* amazed, giving glory and honor to God. It's because of His amazing plan of redemption, sanctification and glorification in the lives of His chosen ones. Those who trust in his one and only Son, Jesus:

"It was revealed to them that they were not serving themselves but you, when they spoke of the things that have now been told you by those who have preached the gospel to you by the Holy Spirit sent from heaven. <u>Even angels long to look into these things.</u>"
—1 Peter 1:12 NIV

OK, so again I digress. It's because there are so many amazing things I want to share with you. We simply don't have enough time in this book to cover it all. Look at that! Even angels long to look in. Angels are a whole other amazing and very real subject. You can't even begin to imagine the things God reveals to those who make Him their refuge. You have a lot to get excited about!

In any case and getting back on point, why is it important to properly understand salvation in Jesus?

Well, we've already discussed *counting the cost*. It's pretty clear valid and reasonable points have been presented as to just where Jesus stands. It's also been revealed some of the attitude and cost He is expecting from you, right?

Just in case, though ... let's remove any cluttered thinking which may be persisting, shall we? Let's do it.

By way of reminder, there was a cost for Jesus when He paid it all to buy you back at a very high price *(His sinless blood)*; isn't that right? There was a cost and it was to redeem you. It was to reconcile you to God, once for all time; did you know this? Of course you know this. You have been alienated from God and Heaven, but then Jesus stepped in to give you hope, right? Absolutely it's right!

Therefore, as you prepare to receive this eternal pardon of a gift, understand God is going to give you a heart which embraces and understands these next few verses. How's that? It's because God is going to change you, supernaturally.

God has a specific plan for you. With all of God—Father, Son and Holy Spirit—being invited to make their home within your heart, you are going to be empowered to *live your life out for another:* Jesus Christ, the One who *saved you!* Your Creator! In God's infinite wisdom, He engineered the salvation package which would provide a means for you having intimate relationship with Him. In depending upon Him and his Spirit as He comforts and leads you, you can now have a meaningful and vibrant love relationship with your Creator!

How does He do this? How does He explain this? How does He encourage you and lead you into all truth?

Simple. We have his Word and God is using me—as an available vessel of His—to convey His truth to you. Can you begin to see the intimacy of this thing? God is the Potter, you are the clay. He is Spirit and establishes intimacy with us when we invite Him in to be united with ourselves; a spirit. Dead spirits need life and since God is Life and Jesus is God, dead spirits are *re-born* into living spirits. *That's you, Heaven-bounder!* This union by nature is a new nature; *one entirely new creation.*

FAITH, MAN. FAITH! You don't get to Heaven rejecting everything God has said and designed for your redemption plan, right? You can't buy this, either. You can't go and just *buy* God and a pass into Heaven. Aren't you glad? God's love is free and His name is Jesus!

In this next section, I'm going to provide you with some word pictures. These should assist you in considering another angle on this whole *God and you thing*, OK? *Let's hop to it!*

You were designed for faith. Did you ever learn about God promising Abraham and Sarah a son Isaac in their senior citizen years? Did you know Abraham was 100 years old and Sarah was 90 years old when God showed them His favor and promise? Everything God is offering to you today, including Heaven, lies solely on your willingness to believe Him. In another word, to trust what He says as truth.

Once you commit to trusting what God says, you will be transformed. Your spiritual bank account will go from hellfire red into a radiant white light. Just look what God did when Abraham trusted Him:

"For if Abraham were justified by works, he has something in which to boast; but not before God. For what says the scripture? <u>Abraham believed God, and it was counted unto him for righteousness</u>. Now to him that works is the reward not reckoned of grace, but of debt. But <u>to him that works not, but believes on him that justifies the ungodly, his faith is counted for righteousness</u>."
—Romans 4:2-5 KJ2000

Bam! Eternal lotto! Ungodly, guilty criminals declared innocent by trusting what God says. Self-righteous people have a hard time getting saved because they are holding onto their filthy rags. This isn't you anymore though, right? No way!

What does God say you need to do to be righteous? Jesus indicated He is God in the flesh and you need to trust on Him, yes? Well? *Whatchyoo gonna do?* Keep up with that silly, old game of trying to *earn* God's favor? No! You're gonna receive Jesus and let Him take you to places you have never been to before, right? Yeah!

Purity, obedience. Faith. Trust. Holiness. Righteousness. Salvation. Sanctification. Justification. Relationship. Love. Favor. Forgiveness. *Man, it doesn't stop I'm tellin' ya!* God's Holy Spirit is ready to unite with you to finish this thing out and take you home. Are you ready?

Like Abraham and Sarah, God wants to do the impossible in your life, as well. He's going to remove the hurdle of getting into Heaven based upon your own efforts. Instead, He's going to seat you right next to Him—in the *heavenlies*—as you live out your real purpose on this planet. Sound good?

So, I promised you we'd cover this God and you thing with some word pictures earlier, right? You thought I forgot. Or maybe I caused you to forget with all of this other stuff is probably more likely the case; maybe?

Whatever the case, let's dive into it real quick then, OK?

What is your purpose? Why surrender to Jesus? Why have relationship with God? Why shouldn't you *self-direct* your life versus God, or this Jesus person?

You have been purchased at a high price, friend. God's Son's sinless, perfect blood to take away your sins before a holy God, remember?

God is spirit and you are His workmanship. As a uniquely engineered clay vessel, you were designed to be filled with and governed by God's Spirit. God sees everything before it occurs because He's not restricted by time, right? Correct! He is not confined to this time-space dimension as we currently are confined to it. But you see, this is where it gets good!

When you receive Jesus as your Lord and Savior, you invite God's Spirit to live inside you. God is then able to capitalize upon your free-will by rewarding your faith. He can give you insight about *all* things. Spiritual truths which are eternal truths. He is the Spirit of Truth, so once you invite Him in, this is what you get!

When you give yourself to God and He comes into your heart and life, He shows you that you were made for so much more than what this world is offering. He re-instates respect for yourself and directs you in how to possess your vessel. For example, we read:

"But he that is joined unto the Lord is one spirit. Flee fornication. Every sin that a man does is outside the body; but he that commits fornication sins against his own body. What? Know you not that your body is the temple of the Holy Spirit who is in you, whom you have of God, and you are not your own? <u>For you are bought with a price: therefore glorify God in your body, and in your spirit, which are God's</u>."
—1 Corinthians 6:17–20 KJ2000

The World isn't guiding and directing you like this. You, yourself, are not even thinking like this when you are off on your own, making up your own moral code; are you? You are daily cognizant of glorifying God with your body? Are you sure?

Here's the deal. Only a life surrendered to God is going to submit to God. You can't submit to God and honor God when Jesus isn't your Lord, my friend. Right? Don't fall for the World's lies. The World doesn't care about you. Look at the Cross. Observe God's perfect demonstration of complete justice and complete mercy. Search out a better solution to your eternal problem and you will never locate one.

After all of this, have you further considered the implications of this relationship with God? A life where you would operate as divinely intended, a special utensil for honorable use in the Master's hand?

In other words, have you considered this?

Is a car—which is manufactured—made so it would drive without a driver? You may offer ideas against this, but try to get the point. Is an office building without a builder? Is that office building intended to be vacant, or occupied? If occupied, then with what: horses or humans?

Again, try to get this point I'm attempting to make. Just as these items were designed for a specific purpose, so indeed are *you* designed for a specific purpose. It isn't to be a *vacant vessel*, devoid of God's Spirit. Nor is God's plan for you to be *occupied with or oppressed by demons*. No, no, no, no, no!

You've seen those people who snap, right? They're always like, *"I don't know what happened. One minute I was standing there and the next minute I was slicing his body up into little pieces."*

I know, I know. The *"experts"* always seem to have the proper diagnosis though, don't they? *"This sexual act and murder is due to a mental disorder."*

Or—*"Well, this is a case of what we call major depression with some fear. Many people suffer from it and they simply snapped. They weren't in their right mind, so who are we to judge? They just need some help."*

Hmm. Is it possible ... and therefore at least on the table, this person just chose to never surrender to Jesus? Could they have simply left their vessel *vacant?* Could this possibly be in the running as a *reasonable explanation* as to why they just *snapped?* Let's check in with the Author of Life, Jesus.

"Jesus, do you have any insight regarding the human body as these bodies relate to the spirit world and crimes against God and another?"

Jesus responds *(via my DNA)*: *"Actually, I have offered some insight in this area. Let's go over to my Word. Turn to Luke Chapter 11, if you would, please."*

"When the unclean spirit is gone out of a man, he walks through dry places, seeking rest; and finding none, he says, I will return unto my house from which I came out. And when he comes, he finds it swept and in order. Then he goes, and takes with him seven other spirits more wicked than himself; and they enter in, and dwell there: and the last state of that man is worse than the first."
—Luke 11:24-26

Look. God has designed you to be *filled with his Holy Spirit!* There's no time to play games with this stuff. You don't want to mess around as if you have it all covered. *You can't have it all covered without Jesus.* Don't deceive yourself and don't allow yourself to be duped by any whispers directing you away from a life surrendered to Jesus. Not a life surrendered to *your opinions.* Not a life surrendered to a *church schedule* and not a life surrendered to some type *church membership.* This isn't a social call, *it's a salvation call!*

Indeed. This is all about a life surrendered to Jesus that will get you home. Are you with me?

That's right, and know this: To be sealed and filled with God's Spirit is *not automatic.* You must invite the Spirit of Christ to make His home within you.

Jesus answered and said to him, "If anyone loves Me, he will keep My word; and My Father will love him, and We will come to him and make Our abode with him."
—John 14:23 NASB

It's a heart *exchange.* It's a *stony heart* swapped out for a *tender heart of flesh.* This is all in the Bible. I'm not making this stuff up. A new heart which desires to *be with* and *enjoy God.* The new heart is being unveiled as you continue reading this book. It's *your rags* for *Christ's riches.* How is this for a deal? Hell canceled, Heaven guaranteed. Not too shabby, right? *I'm with ya! We're on it!*

You became like a child.

JESUS SPEAKS: *"Verily I say unto you,
Except ye be converted, and become as
little children, ye shall not enter into the
kingdom of heaven."*
—Matthew 18:3 KJV

Before you can grow spiritually you must first be
born again—*born of God's Spirit*, right? How can
you be born-again? You are to *trust on Him.*
Who's Him? Jesus.

*Jesus answered and said unto them,
"This is the work of God, that **ye believe
on him** whom he hath sent."*
—John 6:29 KJV
*(i.e. **believe** on = trust on)*

Your full weight *on*, remember? Of course you
do!

In receiving Jesus, you are trusting Him with
your life. In receiving Jesus you are surrendering
your heart to Him. Jesus has a new one He wants
to give you, *anyway.* The new heart is God's plan
in this New Covenant. Jesus has done all the
work, but most people are prideful and think by
doing some type of work, they will inherit
Heaven. *Run for your life from this type of
reasoning and these types of people! It's not
grace!*

Understand: You can only be saved by *grace* though *faith*. God's going to peel back the curtain and show you what is going to happen in your life once you receive Jesus and commit your life into his nail-pierced hands. As we observe this passage, again—watch:

"For <u>by grace</u> you have been saved <u>through faith</u>; and that <u>not of yourselves</u>, it is the <u>gift of God</u>; <u>not</u> as a result of <u>works</u>, so that no one may boast."
—Ephesians 2:8,9

I'm tellin' ya, God has provided the perfect sacrifice in Jesus. The only thing God wants for you is to place your full trust in the finished work of Jesus. When a person has done this, Jesus becomes preeminent in their lives. It takes for you to become like a child to receive this gift though, right? Yes.

You can do this! This is how you got to Heaven. This is an *adventure*. This is *supernatural*. This is *God's plan*. The plan is for you to continue receiving this eternal truth God is pouring *out of me* and *into you*, OK?

Do me a favor. Resist any of the negative talk which may possibly be attempting to surface in your mind right now, OK? This is spiritual warfare and you will learn more about this as you grow.

For now, simply reject any thoughts attempting to draw you away from this truth. The adversary[x] of your soul is the same adversary who whispered lies to Eve in the Garden. That's what started this whole mess, but Jesus came to make things right! God created you. God created the heavens and the earth. What He wants you to do right now is continue to focus on His truth.

Remember, also: There are a lot of *posers* out there. You can oftentimes tell the posers from the real deal though, can't you? Their lips don't match their lifestyle, right? So, what matters *most though* is *your response* to Jesus; not somebody else's. God hasn't forgotten them. Right now, though, He's dealing with you. Why? It's because He's madly in love with you, OK?

So Peter seeing him said to Jesus, "Lord, and what about this man?" Jesus said to him, "If I want him to remain until I come, what is that to you? You follow Me!"
—John 21:21,22

You must first pass *Go*, which is coming into a relationship with Jesus, born then *from above by God's Spirit* and *adopted* into His family. This is the only way to Heaven. It's narrow.

JESUS SPEAKS:

"Strive to enter through the <u>narrow door</u>. For many, I tell you, will seek to enter and will not be able. When once the master of the house has risen and shut the door, and you begin to stand outside and to knock at the door, saying, 'Lord, open to us,' then he will answer you, 'I do not know where you come from.'"
—Luke 13:24,25 ESV

"<u>I am the door</u>: by me if any man enter in, he shall be saved, and shall go in and out, and find pasture."
—John 10:9 KJV
(i.e. "I am the gate ...")

"Enter through the <u>narrow gate</u>; for the gate is wide and the way is broad that leads to destruction, and there are many who enter through it."
—Matthew 7:13 NASB
(i.e. "I am the gate ...")

Once you are adopted as God's child and become a new creature in Christ, the other book titles in this *Bible Insights Collection* would make sense and be applicable to you.

Please do not attempt to pass *Go* without first being born again. You must receive Christ and choose to follow Him, first. Count the cost. God wants your stony heart so He can give you a new, tender one to finish this thing out. You'll never make it without the new heart and this new heart, while free from God as a gift, is only procured when you trust Christ with your life, OK? *Critical stuff.* You are going to get these things right, though, because this is all about *How You Got To Heaven. Let's keep things on track!*

You called out. Wise men still seek Him. True humility is who you are before God. You've heard of all those stories from perturbed wives conveying how their husbands never stop for directions, right? There's a cost to pride. Consequences are part of every choice; some good, some bad. In the case of Heaven, make no doubt about it. There's *Hell to pay* for the proud.

It doesn't matter where you are, today. It doesn't matter for what reason or reasons you have avoided calling out to Jesus to save you. God is full of mercy and forgiveness. He *superabounds* in grace. Where sin exists, God's grace s*uperabounds. Never forget it!*

What is required for sinners to become citizens of Heaven? How did *you* get to Heaven? Let's check in with God, again:

> *"Call to Me and I will answer you, and I will tell you great and mighty things, which you do not know."*
> —Jeremiah 33:3 NASB

###

> *"And it shall come to pass that everyone who <u>calls upon the name of the Lord</u> shall be saved."*
> —Acts 2:21 ESV

So, absolutely. You called out. Heaven is filled with people who called out to Jesus and Hell is filled with people who didn't. It's the math we are faced with in a fallen, sinful and adulterous world. People are adulterers because they have lifted the skirt of their lives to the World and rejected God.

Not you, though. God has been breaking through with you, hasn't He? His truth is just no match for anybody or anything. His truth pierces right through the lies. His creation as evidence screams, *"Creator!"* and His love daily penetrates hearts from the blood-soaked cross and empty tomb.

Jesus is the real deal and you have come to realize He was much more than a great teacher. He's the risen God in flesh and He's reaching out to *you*. Get ready to call out to and upon Him. He has everything you truly will ever need.

You got born twice. Remember? We looked at this earlier. You knew early on this was part of it and there's nothing about it which should cause you to be fearful. Stop being concerned with what others say above what God says, right? We covered *this*, as well. What you need to be fearful of is *not having God directing your life*, right?

When you draw near to God, God draws near to you. The whole issue is your alienation from God because of sin. This is why we are here, because the sin issue has been dealt with by Jesus. You simply need to receive this gift and let it transform you, forever. It starts with a new birth. Remember what Jesus said?

> **"Do not be amazed that I said to you, 'You must be born again.'"**
> —John 3:7 NASB

If we read the rest of what God is saying in context, we see it's all about His love for you in the Person of Jesus, God the Son. Let's read to make sure we get the bigger picture. This is critical. It comes right after Jesus informs us we must be born again.

Most importantly, when you see the word, "world," insert your name because it's the real deal. God is speaking this to you specifically—right now. It's neither a game nor my opinion. It's true this is intended for you. He knows the number of hairs on your head. He formed you in your mother's womb. He knew you'd be reading this book. Keep your focus on all He's saying, here. It'll all come together for you as God continues to open the eyes of your heart. Ready? Go.

"For God so loved the world, that he gave his only begotten Son, that whoever believes in him should not perish, but have everlasting life. For God sent not his Son into the world to condemn the world; but that the world through him might be saved. He that believes on him is not condemned: but he that believes not is condemned already, because he has not believed in the name of the only begotten Son of God. And this is the condemnation, that light is come into the world, and men loved darkness rather than light, because their deeds were evil. For every one that does evil hates the light, neither comes to the light, lest his deeds should be reproved. But he that does truth comes to the light, that his deeds may be made manifest, that they are worked in God."
—John 3:16-21 AKJV

And where does God reveal to us how to become His child by adoption? It's in John's gospel, also. Earlier, in chapter one. Plant your trust firmly on this because we're going to get you home as you hold onto God's promises. Ready once again? Go.

*"But as many **as received him**, **to them gave he power to become the sons of God**, even to them that believe on his name: Which were born, not of blood, nor of the will of the flesh, nor of the will of man, but of God."*
—John 1:12,13 AKJV

Other translations have this as *"children of God."* Same thing, my friend. *Sons* are *children of God* and *daughters* are *children of God*. Sons, daughters, children. God's very own offspring by the specific, exclusive way of those who *"receive him."* This is how you get born again and make it to Heaven. *Cha-ching!* Jesus paid the price so the Judge could legally dismiss your case. You can accept the Pardon and walk away from the court room declared *totally innocent* in the eyes of God.

This is amazing news! You need only receive Him. Are you getting ready? *You were born for this moment in time. If God be for you, who can be against you? Destiny man, destiny! God's rescue mission is in full effect!*

Ready? Set? Get sealed! My friend, it's time. God has a call upon your life. Nobody is more worthy and loving than Jesus. We've covered what we've needed for you to make sense enough of this to take this step of childlike faith towards the One who gave it all to you, haven't we?

Yes! We have and I'm so very excited for you. There are things you still cannot see as to why this is going to blow your mind and eternity. I'm likely more excited about it than you are because I've been walking in this abundance for a decent amount of time. I know what it's like to put every single thing aside and draw near to God for what I needed most: life.

So, while you cannot see all of those magnificent things, yet—you shall. God has arranged this specific time for a very specific creation of His; you!

He isn't learning anything. He knows the number of days you have left and knows what you are going to choose. Both you and I know it's going to be a choice for Jesus and Heaven, though. Right?

Yeah! You know it! You aren't *too young* to surrender to Jesus and you are not *too old* to surrender to Jesus. These past years wasted, God is about to restore back to you!

GOD: *"And <u>I will restore to you the years</u> <u>that the swarming locust has eaten</u>, the crawling locust, and the consuming locust, and the cutting locust, my great army which I sent among you. And you shall eat in plenty, and be satisfied, and <u>praise the name of the LORD your God,</u> <u>who has dealt wondrously with you: and</u> <u>my people shall never be ashamed</u>."*
—Joel 2:25,26 KJ2000

God has restored the years the locust has eaten! Those wasted years trying to live apart from God. *Yes, those!* It is God who holds time and eternity in His hands, right? So, who better to restore your lost and wasted years?

This is why it's not too late. Nicodemus was up in years, clinging to his religious activity and church attendance, self-righteousness—ready to share his resume before God as to why he *should* have eternal life.

Even still, Jesus bypassed all of this and penetrated his soul by informing him he must be born-again. Jesus cut through it all and manages to restore all of that man's years of religious toil in *one, fell swoop!*

Know this: You also aren't *too good* to come to God for forgiveness and you aren't *too bad* to come to God for forgiveness, either. The playing field is even. We read:

> *"For <u>everyone</u> has sinned; <u>we all</u> <u>fall short</u> of God's glorious standard."*
> —Romans 3:23 NLT

But you know what? Jesus died in your place and rose from death for specific purposes. Care to know a few? I know you do, because it's all good.

Jesus came to make you a child of God. He came to transform you from a *sinner* into a *son* or *daughter*. Being a sinner is now going to be a thing of the past for you. Jesus has your new identity and it's not, *"sinner!"*

No. One of God's reasons for becoming a man and dying in your place is to give you a completely new identity. In receiving Jesus by inviting Him in, you are receiving God into your life. God makes His home in hearts because He gives out *new hearts* under this agreement. He knows you need one to get to Heaven and He's ready and willing to give it to you when you accept Jesus, in faith.

By having God reside within you, the old you dies and the new you is a mighty warrior, because God is a warrior! Jesus came to defeat death, sin and the enemy of your soul. He was victorious at the cross some 2,000 years or so, ago.

When you step into this thing, the power of sin is going to be *broken* in your life. As a newborn babe in Christ, you're gonna learn to crawl before you walk. You'll crave the milk of God's Word to cause you to grow stronger in your faith, too.

"Like newborn babies, you must <u>crave pure spiritual milk</u> so that you will <u>grow</u> into a full experience of salvation. Cry out for this nourishment,"
—1 Peter 2:2 NLT

All the while, you will have the light of life—God's Holy Spirit. Jesus is that light. God is light, in Him is no darkness. God in you is light, my friend! This is what you have been needing and looking for. You have found it. It's a relationship with God, through Jesus. Are you ready to receive Him? Let me check.

Hmmm. Yep, you certainly appear to be ready to ask Him into your heart to wipe away every single sin and crime, past, present and future; aren't ya? Oh, man! This is good. God is *sooo* ready for you. He desires to be your Heavenly Father! He's amazing. *C'mon. Let's get this done! Now is the time of salvation.* Today is the day you got right with God—once for all time.

Jesus Ascends and Will Return
And when he had spoken these things, while they beheld, he was taken up; and a cloud received him out of their sight. And while they looked steadfastly toward heaven as he went up, behold, two men stood by them in white apparel;

Who also said, "You men of Galilee, why stand you gazing up into heaven? This same Jesus, who is taken up from you into heaven, shall so come in like manner as you have seen him go into heaven."
—Acts 1:9-11 KJ2000

Receive your Pardon. Present yourself to God. Make Heaven your new home.

We're going to do this together, OK? God is Light. In Him is no darkness at all.[xi] How will you ever get Light in your life? Or, will you remain in darkness?
No! Not you, remember? God is Light and Jesus is God ... so? How can you cross over from darkness into The Kingdom of his marvelous Light?

> ### *"In Him was life, and the life was the Light of men."*
> —John 1:4 NASB

You shall receive Him. What more reasonable way to bring light to your darkened soul? Only Jesus is Light, so if you don't have Him, you have no true *enlightenment* or *Light*, right? *Right!*
   Therefore, I'm going to lead the way in order to help you along. If you want to use your own words, you can do so. They should include the main parts of this prayer, though. You're in good hands, though. So, let's just pray, OK?

By the way, there's no need to put this off. Life comes down to choices, right? Life is also brief, as we discussed. Anything trying to get in the way of this is simply an attempt to keep you out of Heaven. Why? It's because there is a battle going on for the souls of people and you are in the middle of this invisible war. The kingdom of darkness is trying to claim your soul. It anticipates your coming so it can swallow you up. *I'm not even kidding.* God has already revealed this in his Word.[xii]

However, you are going to cross over from death to life, today. You know already this is the way. The only One who can help you at your greatest need is the only One who appropriately solved the problem: Jesus.

Full weight, remember? Imputed righteousness, remember? Rags for riches, yes? Life over death, right?

As it is said, "Today, if you hear his voice, do not harden your hearts as in the rebellion."
—Hebrews 3:15 ESV

###

For God says, "At just the right time, I heard you. On the day of salvation, I helped you." Indeed, the 'right time' is now. Today is the day of salvation."
—2 Corinthians 6:2 NLT

Yeah! So, I know I said we were going to pray. So, let's do this right now. We're gonna do coffee or something in Heaven, so we have to make sure we're going to the same place, right? Step out of the boat of your life and onto the water. Pay no mind to the wind and the crashing waves. Instead, fix your eyes upon the anchor for your soul, Jesus Christ. Let's do this.

"God, I admit to You today I have fallen short in so many areas. I have sinned against You and I'm so sorry. I have not put You first and have been busy trying to lead my own life. But You love me and sent Jesus to die for me. You sent Him to make a covenant of everlasting love and forgiveness between You and me. I receive and agree with this covenant— signed in the precious blood of Your Son. After Jesus was crucified, I believe You then raised Him from the dead. I receive it, Lord. I turn now from my sins and sinful lifestyle. I place my full trust in You, Jesus, to guide and lead me into Heaven. I choose this day to follow you all the days of my life. I pray this in Your name Jesus, Amen!"

If you said this prayer and meant it in your heart, God has saved you. You have been born of God's Spirit and *you* are now a child of God. You have a lot to celebrate! God has sealed you with his Spirit.

Do you like the start of a new year? How about the start of a *new life!* That's what I'm *talkin' about!* You have a bunch of amazing stuff going on now, actually. I describe this in more detail through my other *Bible Insights Collection* titles.

As mentioned, your inheritance includes God's Spirit as a *down-payment* on the *new body* you have coming your way. I'm telling you, it's out of this world!

You'll spend the rest of your earthly life discovering all God has done for you and I want to be part of it. We have to stay in touch after this via my on-line presence *(e.g. nowaydude.org, facebook, twitter, etc.)* or through the mail, if you haven't an Internet connection, OK? I want to encourage you as you *grow in Christ!*

Are you excited? You may have felt something, you may have not felt anything. What matters is what God says and He is faithful. When you do what you did, God has taken residence up inside of you because he keeps his Word. As your faith grows, you will come to realize God is in you.

You will also begin to recognize this new journey isn't about relying upon your emotions—as far as whether or not what God says is true or not. This is about placing your complete hope and trust in Jesus as your Savior and Lord. It's also about putting this same type of hope and trust in his Word, the Bible. You know it's true because we covered this earlier, right?

Cool! I told you it was *on*. You ready to finish things up in a bit? We're going to get you off as best we can in this short book. Then, more miracles are going to follow in your life. Sound good? You're certainly right it's good! You have only just begun to experience how good God is. *It's on, it's on, it's on!*

Summary

What happened this chapter?

You got *saved*, that's what happened this chapter! You called out to Jesus and He saved you like He promised He would, right?

You recognized God requires a conversion for an entry into Heaven.

Additionally, you came to acknowledge and embrace this concept of losing your life in order to save it. In losing your life by trusting in Jesus by grace alone through faith alone, you have found your life. You were once lost, but *now you are found!*

All of this was based upon God demonstrating to you how you must have a re-birth for Him to adopt you. God adopted you when you received Jesus into your heart. It wasn't because some fallible person came up with the idea. It's been because the *infallible* God came up with the whole thing and you trusted Him regarding it!

God sealed you for the day of redemption and now calls you one of His own. You are God's offspring. You were once alienated from God, but Jesus stood in the gap and you trusted Him to do so.

Finally, this is why you will now *know* you are going to Heaven.

Previously, you were trusting in yourself to merit Heaven. This was a dead-end and caused you to be unsure—*and rightfully so!* God designed it this way because when you are unsure or forming your opinion on *justification before a holy God* inaccurately, there is hell to pay.

No more hell for you, though! You have settled the matter and have been reconciled unto God *through your faith in Jesus Christ.* Your decision to trust and follow Christ wasn't disingenuous, nor shall your life moving ahead in Christ be! You know the time for playing games is over. This is why you investigated this book. You were tired of being unsure and God used this to give you a new life. Now walk in it with confidence, daily.

Instead of being unsure, you are sure now because your faith isn't in yourself. It's fully in Jesus. This is why you can be assured of Heaven and indeed what God has intended for you. He wants you to be *certain* you *are saved* and *already have a place in Heaven!*

"He that __has the Son__ __has life__; and he __that has not the Son of God__ __has not life__. These things have I written unto you that believe on the name of the Son of God; that __you may know that you have eternal life__, and that you may believe on the name of the Son of God."
—I John 5:12,13

JESUS SPEAKS: *"This is eternal life, that they may know You, the only true God, and Jesus Christ whom You have sent."*
—John 17:3 NASB

"But God, who is rich in mercy, for his great love with which he loved us, Even when we were dead in sins, has made us alive together with Christ, (by grace you are saved;) And has raised us up together, and made us sit together in heavenly places in Christ Jesus: That in the ages to come he might show the exceeding riches of his grace in his kindness toward us through Christ Jesus. For by grace are you saved through faith; and that not of yourselves: it is the gift of God: Not of works, lest any man should boast. For we are his workmanship, created in Christ Jesus unto good works, which God has before ordained that we should walk in them."
—Ephesians 2:4-10 KJ2000

"Created in Christ Jesus" means you haven't just been born of the flesh or the will of man. No! You have also been born of God's Spirit—*born again*—when you made this decision. The decision was to invite Jesus into your heart to reign and rule over your life, willingly. *Amazing! Congratulations!*

"And do not grieve the <u>Holy Spirit of God,</u> <u>with whom you were sealed</u> for the day of redemption."
—Ephesians 4:30 NIV

"And do not bring sorrow to God's Holy Spirit by the way you live. Remember, he has identified you as his own, <u>guaranteeing</u> that you will be saved on the day of redemption."
—Ephesians 4:30 NLT

You *are saved*, you *are being saved* and you *will be saved*. This is *all* based upon your being *born-again* by *receiving Jesus*. It's God's *salvation* plan. It's Good News!

Life Application

1. How do you feel? Does your salvation depend upon how you feel or upon God's Word and what He says? What brought you to this conclusion?

2. Did you expect to be brought to a place where you asked Jesus into your heart to save you? Was it worth your time and worth reading this book?

3. How do you think this chapter will impact the way you live?

No Way, Dude...

Way!

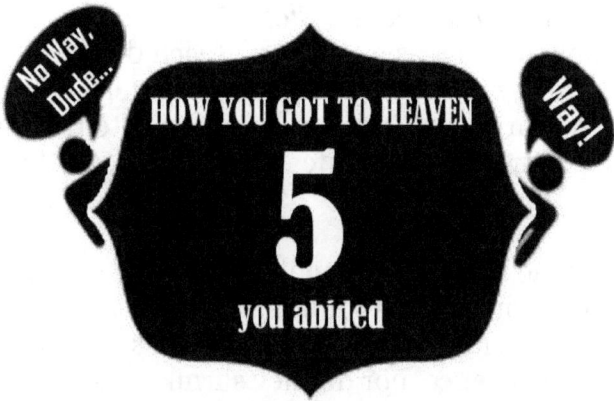

How Did You Get To Heaven?
YOU ABIDED

In Jesus

Each of us can only live one moment and one day at a time. God created you to walk with Him. He created you for Him. There's still a lot to learn. What newborn baby comes out of the womb and says, *"What are you trying to teach me? I've been born for an entire minute."* Or, *"I've been born a whopping fifteen days, already. What can you teach me? Depart from my glorious, omniscient presence!"*

You say, *"That's crazy. Stop."* No, all of the people who act as if God can't teach them anything *need to stop;* right? Absolutely! Our lives apart from God can deceive us into thinking we pretty much have life figured out, can't they? Sure they can.

Yet, who having a rational mind would continue on with this type of thinking? No ... I said, *rational. Ha-ha.* Yes. Rational minds don't deny God's existence, nor do they shrink back in approaching Him for wisdom—through Jesus. Do they?

> **The fool says in his heart, "There is no God."**
> —Psalm 14:1 NIV

"<u>If any of you lack wisdom, let him ask of God</u>, that gives to all men liberally, and upbraides not; and it shall be given him. But let him ask in faith, nothing wavering. For he that wavers is like a wave of the sea driven with the wind and tossed. For let not that man think that he shall receive any thing of the Lord. A double minded man is unstable in all his ways."
—James 1:5-8 AKJV

God even asked Job *(long "o")*—who had gone through some unthinkable trials—to *weigh in* on some matters:

> **Then the LORD answered Job out of the whirlwind and said:**
> **"Who is this that darkens counsel by words without knowledge?**
> **Dress for action like a man;**
> **I will question you, and you make it known to me.**
> **"Where were you when I laid the foundation of the earth?**
> **Tell me, if you have understanding.**
> **Who determined its measurements— surely you know!**
> —Job 38:1-5

"JZ, what are you getting at?"

Abiding, remember? To *abide* means *to remain with, not depart from; continue with.* [xiii]

Well, let's bring it closer to home, then. You got sealed by God's Spirit and are born-again, right? This has been your answer as to how you got to Heaven, right? It's all true, oh so true. You are correct.

And yet, there's further instructions required for how you got to Heaven. They are not strings attached. These instructions are spirit and they are life. The way God set this up was for you to live life and have it *to the full.*

Therefore and in order to do so, God's wisdom and eternal plan has been to save you and me from the pit of hell. He does this by placing our feet upon the solid foundation and Rock of Jesus Christ. It is this same, wise God—Jesus Christ—who is here to reveal further, critical insight to you:

> **Then said Jesus to those Jews who believed on him, "_If_ you continue in my word, _then_ are you my disciples indeed; And you shall know the truth, and the truth shall make you free."**
> —John 8:31:32 KJ2000

Let's look at it again, only this time with a slightly different bit of emphasis:

> **"_If_ you <u>continue in my word</u>, <u>then</u> are you my disciples indeed; And <u>you shall know the truth</u>, and <u>the truth shall make you free</u>."**
> —John 8:31:32 KJ2000

What was it that led you into being able to make a sound, reasonable decision when it came to being born-again? It's been God's Word, right?

"For the word of God is <u>living</u>, and <u>powerful</u>, and <u>sharper than any two-edged sword</u>, piercing even to the dividing asunder of soul and spirit, and of the joints and marrow, and is a discerner of the thoughts and intents of the heart."
—Hebrews 4:12 NLT

We also know God's Word *is truth* from an earlier chapter, right? Right! God is lovingly instructing you how to always *know the truth* and how to *always be free*. It's right up there. Go ahead. Read it, again.

You now have answers. You came into this book seeking and since God is a *Rewarder* of those who diligently seek Him, you found answers. Answers on how you got to Heaven. Answers about knowing truth and being free. It's pretty darn good time spent; no? Hell canceled, Heaven secured. Truth winning out over lies. Bondage to freedom. Not too shabby.

So, if you have really been converted because you became like a child ... if you have really been born of God's Spirit, then you will abide or *remain in* and *not depart from* Jesus and His words, right? I mean, this is a reasonable conclusion based upon what we've covered thus far, right?

You know it! You *have been set free* and Jesus—along with what He says—is going to continue to make you free. So remember, you have one mission every day above all other missions in life: abide in Jesus, abide in Jesus, abide in Jesus. *Remain in Jesus and His words, depart not from Jesus and His words. Remain with, continue with Jesus. Then and only then shall I know the truth and shall I be free, forever!* Know it. Live it. Represent it. *God is with you! God is in you!*

Jesus gives you power, authority and real fruit. Living with and for God in Jesus is supernatural! God is spirit and He's now in you! You backed out of the prayer? Go back! Do not collect two hundred dollars—or in this case, Heaven—until you commit your life to Christ. Receive Him, my friend! You know this isn't a game. No more lame excuses, remember?

OK, so where were we? Oh yeah. Your new, Heaven-bound life.

So what is it, again? It's Christ *in you*, the hope of glory! God is living in you. How is this ever going to be boring and unfulfilling? *It's not, silly!*

In losing your life to Jesus, you have *found your life*. Jesus promised and He doesn't lie, right? Nobody could prove Him guilty of sin and nobody has since. Why? You know why. He's the blemish-less Lamb of God, slain as the perfect sacrifice for you. In your place, remember? Yeah! Amazing love, right?

Think about it. Jesus said He *is the Life*. Then, you invited Life *in* when you invited Jesus into your heart. Make sense? Good.

Now, we're not going to cover the power and authority aspect of your salvation in detail right now. However, you can learn more about your true identity in the other *Bible Insights Collection* titles, as mentioned. For now, I want to make sure you at least know some of the basics of the *new you*.

You have power in Jesus. In accepting Christ, *the power of sin is broken* in your life. Jesus took care of it at the Cross. So, if you ever have the experience after this conversion where you think you may be living an old, sinful lifestyle ... you will be served well to gain a proper understanding of grace.

Why so? This is because if you are truly under grace, sin *will not* be your master. Jesus will be. When Jesus isn't preeminent in your life, sin will be. It's simple Kingdom math. It's God's math and God's reality. The only reality. Only if you are deceiving yourself with your commitment would sin reign and not Jesus, right?

A simple change of mind *(i.e. repentance)* can change your situation. In having your lips match your lifestyle, God gives you power. Also, when genuinely walking in faith you have the power to do what is right before God; not what is wrong. Jesus didn't save you to do wrong. He saved you to do what is right, which is *trusting on Him*, remember? And when you trust on Him, you have power over sin. You have power over sin because you trust Jesus handled it at the Cross. You *trust* God *loves you* because He went out of His way to demonstrate that love to you about 2,000 years ago at the Cross, right? Right!

Jesus puts his money where his mouth is, right? You are now going to do the same thing because when you invited Him in, the *old you* was crucified with Him. *Behold, all things <u>are become new</u>!* Now, you have *His life* and you live *your life by faith in the Son of God.* This is what it means to *abide* in one, major sense. *Are you good with this? Good!*

You have authority in Jesus. If you haven't noticed—but something tells me you have—you live in a world filled with lies, murder, rape, betrayal, war, unfaithfulness, deception, corruption and all sorts of evil!

As you grow in Jesus, you will come to further realize the importance of having authority in any given situation. Instead of living by the dictates of your flesh, you are now to be *led by God's Spirit.* He's replaced your *old nature, your old heart, your old mind and your old spirit.*[xiv] This part about *being led* is what now distinguishes you from those who are still lost in darkness and alienated from God.

Religious people and atheists are not *Spirit-led*; they are *flesh-led*. Why? It's because they still *trust in themselves* and what they *do*. Again, this is not faith. Therefore, God's Spirit is not leading them. Who are not led by God's Spirit? Certainly not God's children. *Certainly not you*, now. Validate it. Here it is. Isn't it amazing how the sword of God's Word cuts through all the confusion?

> *"For those who are led by the Spirit of God are the children of God."*
> —Romans 8:14 NIV

So, who are the ones cutting through the lies because they have God in them and God as their Heavenly Father? *God's children. Correct!* Who are God's children? Those *and only those who are led by his Spirit.* Let this serve as just one example where God is specifying—in a very clear way—not all people are his children.

If you want to be God's child, you *must be born-again* by receiving Jesus. God can then *lead you by his Spirit* because there is no other way to the Father *except through Jesus,* according to Jesus.

Therefore, understand that since you are *now alive in Christ* and a child of God, the battlefield for the souls of men rages on!

"For we are not fighting against flesh-and-blood enemies, but against evil rulers and authorities of the unseen world, against mighty powers in this dark world, and against evil spirits in the heavenly places."
—Ephesians 6:12 NLT

Authority matters and you now have it. Aren't you glad about this? Your offensive weapons are prayer and the Sword of the Spirit—which is the Word of God. I have been wielding the Sword *all throughout this book* because this is the weapon God has given to me. Has it not *already* cut through some lies in your life? *Scoreboard!*

God is victorious over these evil rulers in the Person of Jesus Christ. Now that you have invited Him in to save you, you are going to finish this thing out fighting *from* a position of victory—*not for it*—as you trust in Jesus.

Crazy, isn't it? Maybe it's crazy, but it's true! *God is a Warrior and He's amazing! Go Jesus!*

You have lasting, genuine fruit in Jesus.

Have you ever seen those bowls of plastic fruit? At first glance, you get excited because they look good enough to eat, right? Then, you become immediately disappointed because all you have in front of you is hard, inedible, plastic fruit. Right?

You know it! This isn't cool, is it? Why not some nice, fresh and satisfying fruit, right? *Yeah! I'm hungry.* I want to get into something good! Where's the *real fruit?*

Well, if you can see the logic in this, why would it be unreasonable for the Author of Life to enjoy real fruit, as well? Let me confirm something with you: *God is all about it!*

JESUS SPEAKS: "I am the true vine, and my Father is the vine dresser. Every branch in me that bears not fruit he takes away: and every branch that bears fruit, he prunes it, that it may bring forth more fruit.

Now you are clean through the word which I have spoken unto you. Abide in me, and I in you. As the branch cannot bear fruit of itself, except it abide in the vine; no more can you, except you abide in me.

I am the vine, you are the branches: <u>He that abides in me, and I in him, the same brings forth much fruit: for without me you can do nothing.</u> If a man abides not in me, he is cast forth as a branch, and is withered; and men gather them, and cast them into the fire, and they are burned.

If you <u>abide in me, and my words abide in you</u>, you shall ask what you will, and it shall be done unto you. In this is my Father glorified, that <u>you bear much fruit</u>; so shall you be my disciples."
—John 15:1-8 KJ2000

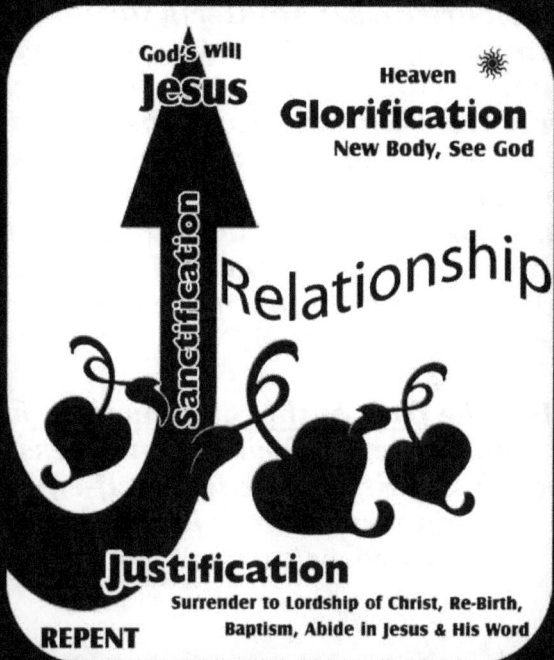

God's will
Jesus

Heaven
Glorification
New Body, See God

Sanctification

Relationship

Justification
Surrender to Lordship of Christ, Re-Birth,
Baptism, Abide in Jesus & His Word

REPENT

"I am the vine, you are the branches; he who abides in Me and I in him, he bears much fruit, for apart from Me you can do nothing.

If anyone does not abide in Me, he is thrown away as a branch and dries up; and they gather them, and cast them into the fire and they are burned." (John 15:5-6)

"Now the <u>works of the flesh</u> are manifest, which are these; Adultery, fornication, impurity, licentiousness, Idolatry, witchcraft, hatred, strife, jealousy, wrath, selfishness, divisions, heresies, Envyings, murders, drunkenness, revelings, and such like: of which I tell you beforehand, as I have also told you in time past, that they who do such things shall not inherit the kingdom of God."

"But the <u>fruit of the Spirit</u> is love, joy, peace, longsuffering, gentleness, goodness, faith, Meekness, self-control: against such there is no law."
—Galatians 5 19-23 KJ2000

\#\#\#

"Therefore, my brethren, you also have become dead to the law by the body of Christ; that you should be married to another, even to him who is raised from the dead, that <u>we should bring forth fruit unto God</u>. For when we were in the flesh, the passions of sins, which were by the law, did work in our members to bring forth fruit unto death. But now we are delivered from the law, being dead to that in which we were held; that we should serve in <u>newness of spirit, and not in the oldness of the letter.</u>"
—Romans 7:4-6 KJ2000

Only a new root is gonna change the fruit!
Leave behind the mindset of trying to please God
by and with what you do—as it relates to *both
how and why* you now merit Heaven. It's not
about right doing, but right believing. When you
believe right, you will do right.

Branches don't struggle on the vine to pop out
grapes; do they? Heck no. Those branches abide
in the vine and produce much fruit, right?

Absolutely. So, by *abiding in Jesus and this
truth*, you *will bear fruit* unto God. *Real, lasting
fruit.* Not that cheap and fake counterfeit fruit.
Keep it real, yo!

By staying in the Spirit. In abiding in Jesus, you stayed in the Spirit. How else even more specifically will you stay in the Spirit? You will keep your mind on the things of the Spirit.

Since God's Word is spirit and truth, you have wisely decided to let God pour his truth into you via his Word; the Holy Bible. Right? You can read it, listen to it, *watch and listen* to it—whatever works for you. Whatever it takes because as we discussed earlier: the only way to replace something with the other is to continually pour the new thing in. Make sense?

Correct! So, what do you need to pour into your mind and heart in this world filled with lies and deception? Exactly. God's Word. Stay in the Spirit!

"For the mind <u>set on the flesh is death</u>, but the mind <u>set on the Spirit is life and peace</u>,"
—Romans 8:6 NASB

Also, keep in mind: God has revealed to us people can *actually deceive themselves*. With your being on your new, narrow path to Heaven ... *such is not the case for you!* We read:

"Be not deceived; God is not mocked: for whatsoever a man soweth, that shall he also reap. For he that soweth to his flesh shall of the flesh reap corruption; but he that soweth to the Spirit shall of the Spirit reap life everlasting."
—Galatians 6:7,8 KJV

Some of this may sound new to you. Whether or not you have heard it, know this and be reminded of this: If anyone be found in Christ, they are a *new creation*. Old things have passed away. Behold, all things are become *new!*

This is why just as any *loving* parent trains up a child in the way they *should* go, so has your Heavenly Father begun to train you up! He's setting you off in the right direction with all you have learned from Him, thus far. He also offers instruction and wisdom like this:

> **"And be not conformed to this world: but <u>be ye transformed by the renewing of your mind</u>, that ye may prove what is that good, and acceptable, and perfect, will of God."**
> —Romans 12:2 KJV

Stay in the Spirit!

Your old self died. Recognize Christ *crucified* your old self at the Cross around 2,000 years ago. *Crucifixion* is an *event*, not a process. On the other hand, sanctification is an *event and a process*. God sets you apart, then God changes you with his Spirit and Word. Sanctification is typically viewed as a process, but don't forget: When you received Christ, God immediately made you a new creation and set you apart unto Himself, OK? When you received Him, you *supernaturally stepped into this* and capitalized on what He accomplished for you.

They ain't sellin' this at the clubs or the games, man! The best things in life are free!

Additionally, God now calls you to *throw off* that old, crucified nature and to be clothed in Christ. This is why you also *threw off and buried that old you*—directly in obedience to your loving, liberating Heavenly Father.

God has redeemed you in the Person of God the Son, Jesus. You can learn more and *I encourage you to learn more* about this ongoing discovery of the new you. Look into one of the *Bible Insights Collection* books on *nowaydude.org*. There are enough reading options to go around for both guys *and* gals.

Summary

You continually know you are saved because you *abide in Jesus and his Word,* the Bible. Jesus is God. All Scripture is God-breathed. Jesus is the Word, incarnate. The Holy Bible is God's written Word. *Right?* Right!

So, when you *believe* Jesus, you abide in Him and his words. This is how you experience truth and authentic freedom. *They go hand in hand!*

Make sure you *daily abide* so you will *daily* be reminded that you now have *power, authority and lasting, true fruit* in Jesus. You want to be fruitful, don't you? I know you do! So: *remain in, depart not from* ... Jesus. Make sense? Absolutely it makes sense. We're singing off the same sheet of music, now—aren't we!

Life Application

1. Have you ever had *power* in life to do what is right before God? *(i.e. trust Jesus over self, avoid sin, etc?)* How or why is this relevant?

2. Have you ever had *authority* over *powers and principalities of the unseen realm?* Who provides to you this authority?

3. What about the ability to produce true, real and lasting fruit ... unto God? Are you able to do this on your own, according to the words of Jesus? What changes in your thinking can you make to align yourself with this?

4. What are some ways you can *stay in the Spirit?*

5. Who lives now? Who died? How might this impact your relationship with God in the ongoing area of *trust?*

"My old self has been crucified with Christ. It is no longer I who live, but Christ lives in me. So I live in this earthly body by trusting in the Son of God, who loved me and gave himself for me."
—Galatians 2:20 NLT

HOW YOU GOT TO **HEAVEN**

Conclusion

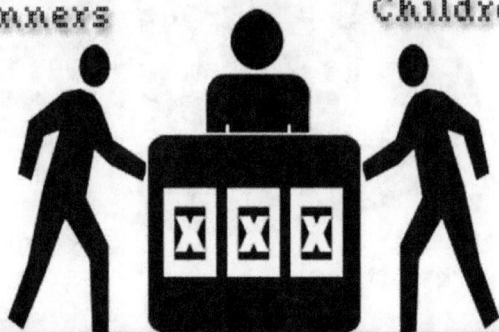

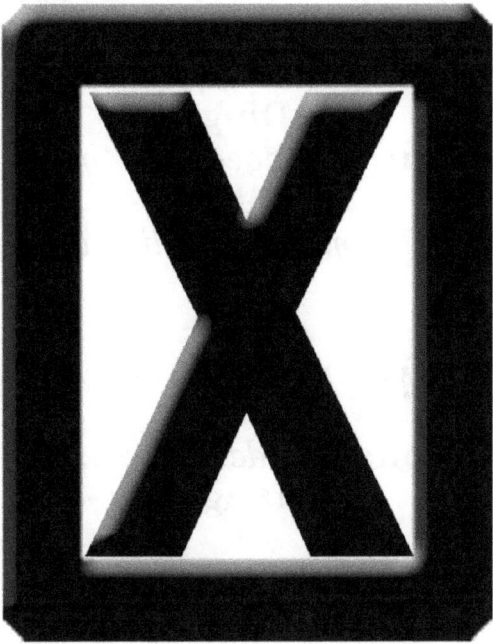

How Did You Get To Heaven?

You: *"I had ears to hear!?"*
Ding!
You: *"I changed My Mind!?"*
Ding!
You: *"I stopped gambling with my soul!?"*
Ding!
You: *"I experienced a conversion!??"*
Ding!
You: *"I abided in Jesus!?"*
Ding!

YOU CAME TO KNOW GOD THROUGH JESUS

<u>"This is eternal life, that they may know You, the only true God, and Jesus Christ whom You have sent."</u>
—John 17:3

Jesus said unto her, I am the resurrection, and the life: he that believeth in me, though he were dead, yet shall he live:
—John 11:25 KJV

Religious activity or doing good deeds—apart from living a passionate life in and for Jesus—is just fake fruit. What matters is a *new creation!*[xv]

Now on the last day, the great day of the feast, Jesus stood and cried out, saying, "If anyone is thirsty, let him come to Me and drink."
—John 7:37 NASB

KNOW THIS: Jesus stepped in and protected the *sinner* as others were preparing to stone her for the act of adultery. Jesus is your *shield* and so much more!

When Jesus had lifted himself up, and saw none but the woman, he said unto her, "Woman, where are those your accusers? Has no man condemned you?" She said, "No man, Lord. And Jesus said unto her, Neither do I condemn you: go, and sin no more."
—John 8:10,11 KJ2000

Cling to Him and what He says! Even his mother, Mary, knew this:
"But his mother told the servants, 'Do whatever he tells you.'"
—John 2:5 NLT

Speaking of Mary, a *truly blessed woman,* Jesus wants you to *keep it real.* Make sure you hear his words clearly. Place everything in its proper order of *priority.* We read:

> **"While Jesus was saying these things, one of the women in the crowd raised her voice and said to Him, 'Blessed is the womb that bore You and the breasts at which You nursed.' But He said, <u>'On the contrary, blessed are those who hear the word of God and observe it.'"</u>**
> —Luke 11:27,28 NASB

So, let's continue to observe God's Word that we might become wise. Amen?

Even though Jesus is coming back as Judge, He came in order *to save!* Never forget the compassion and saving power of Jesus. He died for *sinners* so they could become something more: *Sons of God! Daughters of God! Transformation!*

Jesus takes you as you are—but He loves you far too much to let you remain living as you have been. Jesus first *catches* His fish, then He *cleans them.* Jesus has made you clean.

God's Word will continue to cleanse you. *Don't run away from the mirror. Don't run away from the shower!* Else, you're gonna *stink!* Right? You will, I promise!

Imagine a newborn baby sprawled out in the middle of the street, *starving*. It's not a pretty picture. This is a picture of *you* living in the World without God's Word, the Bible. Babies need milk, so drink up and grow strong so you can move onto solid food!

Instead of being a stinky, malnourished baby ... choose instead to be that of a *pleasant fragrance now unto God, your Heavenly Papa.*

"For we are the aroma of Christ to God among those who are being saved and among those who are perishing, to one a fragrance from death to death, to the other a fragrance from life to life."
—2 Corinthians 2:15,16 ESV

Fantastic! Go now and *abide in Jesus and his Word.* You are no longer *of this World.* You are *in* but not *of.* Got it? *Good!*

So, there it is. This has been all about: *How You Got To Heaven.* "*No Way, Dude,*" you say?
Way!

Heaven is your destination and we're likely going to look back at this as we praise God. We'll praise Him for how He tracked you down and rescued you in Jesus, OK? *Yes! Go ahead and book it!*

This then means our time—at least in this particular book's journey—has just about come to a close.

I'm so privileged God has used me to show you how you got to Heaven. It's all about Jesus and it's all about His love—specifically for *you!* Not just for *anybody;* but for *you! You* are a *unique creation of His* with your very own fingerprint and specially engineered DNA. *What a Creator! What a Savior! What a Friend you have in Jesus!* It's not some trivial slogan. It's *eternal truth,* my *dear transformed soul!*

In closing, do me a favor. Will you? Decide to memorize this verse below and let it encourage you from this point on until you meet Jesus face to face. You will be blessed. You already are blessed. Therefore, *so long for now!*

JESUS SPEAKS:
 "The kingdom of heaven is like treasure hidden in a field, which a man found and covered up. Then in his joy he goes and sells all that he has and buys that field."
—Matthew 13:44 ESV

Illustrations

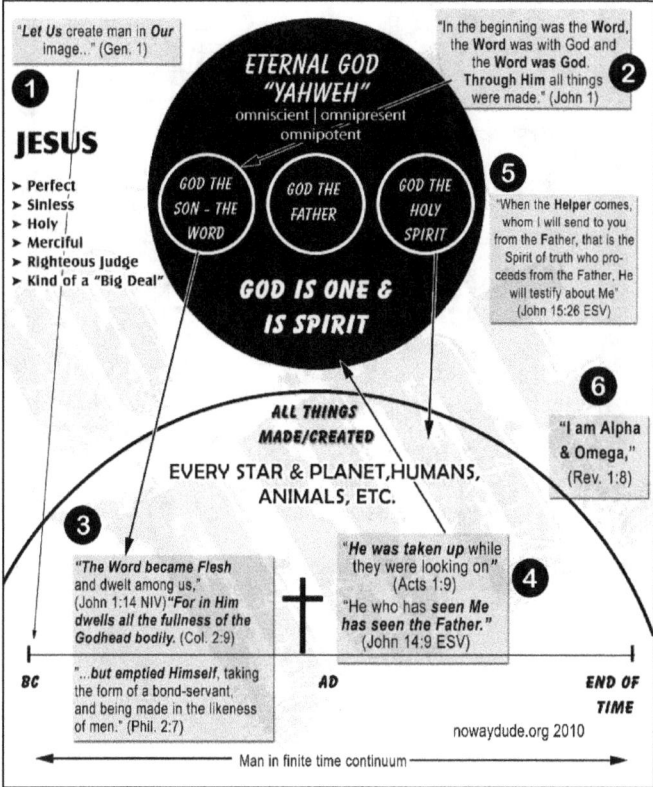

"Let Us create man in Our image..." (Gen. 1)

1

JESUS

➤ Perfect
➤ Sinless
➤ Holy
➤ Merciful
➤ Righteous Judge
➤ Kind of a "Big Deal"

ETERNAL GOD
"YAHWEH"
omniscient | omnipresent omnipotent

GOD THE SON - THE WORD

GOD THE FATHER

GOD THE HOLY SPIRIT

GOD IS ONE & IS SPIRIT

"In the beginning was the **Word**, the **Word** was with God and the **Word was God**. **Through Him** all things were made." (John 1)

2

5

"When the **Helper** comes, whom I will send to you from the Father, that is the Spirit of truth who proceeds from the Father, He will testify about Me" (John 15:26 ESV)

6

"I am Alpha & Omega," (Rev. 1:8)

ALL THINGS MADE/CREATED

EVERY STAR & PLANET, HUMANS, ANIMALS, ETC.

3

"The Word became Flesh and dwelt among us," (John 1:14 NIV) *"For in Him dwells all the fullness of the Godhead bodily.* (Col. 2:9)

"He was taken up while they were looking on" (Acts 1:9)

"He who has **seen Me** has seen the Father." (John 14:9 ESV)

4

"...but emptied Himself, taking the form of a bond-servant, and being made in the likeness of men." (Phil. 2:7)

BC

AD

END OF TIME

nowaydude.org 2010

⬅ Man in finite time continuum ➡

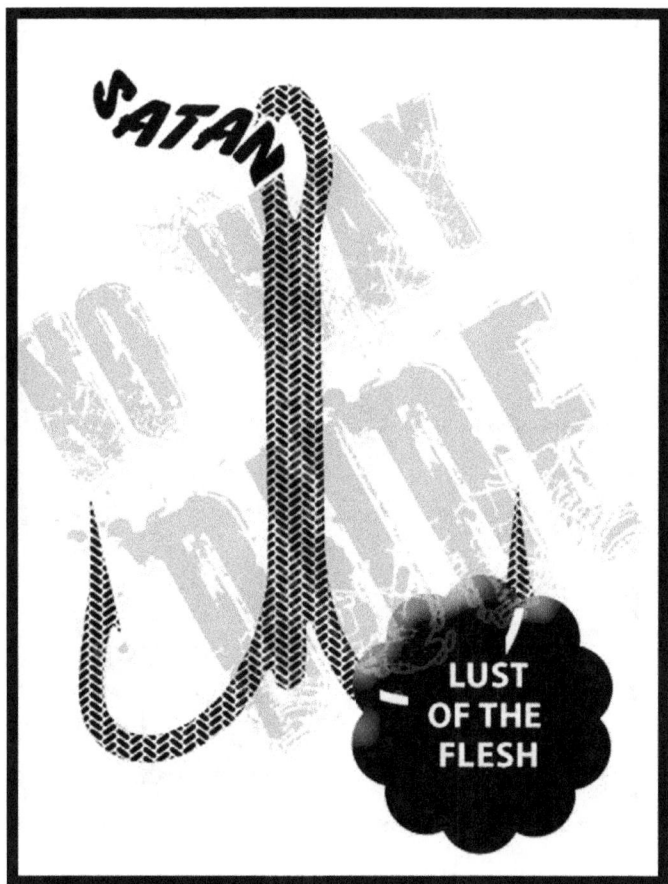

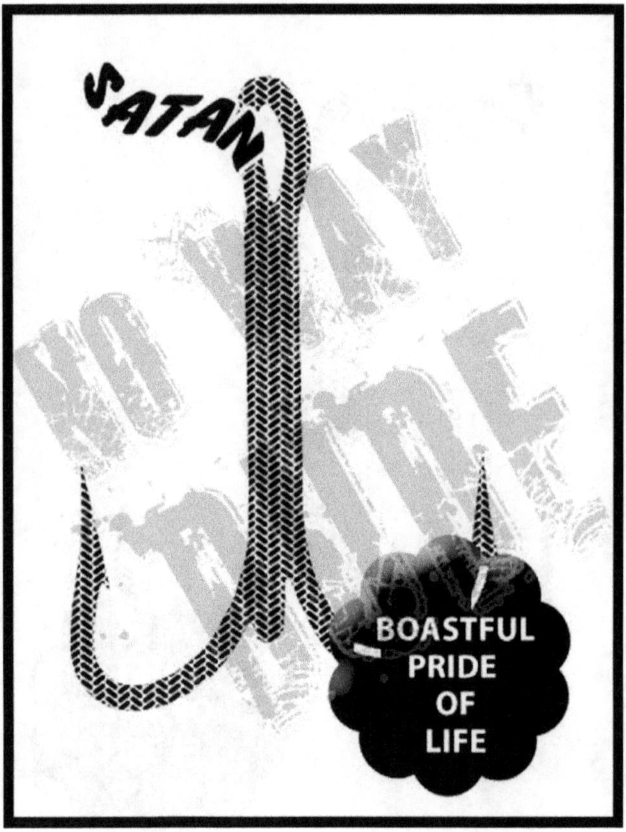
SATAN
NO WAY
PRIDE
BOASTFUL PRIDE OF LIFE

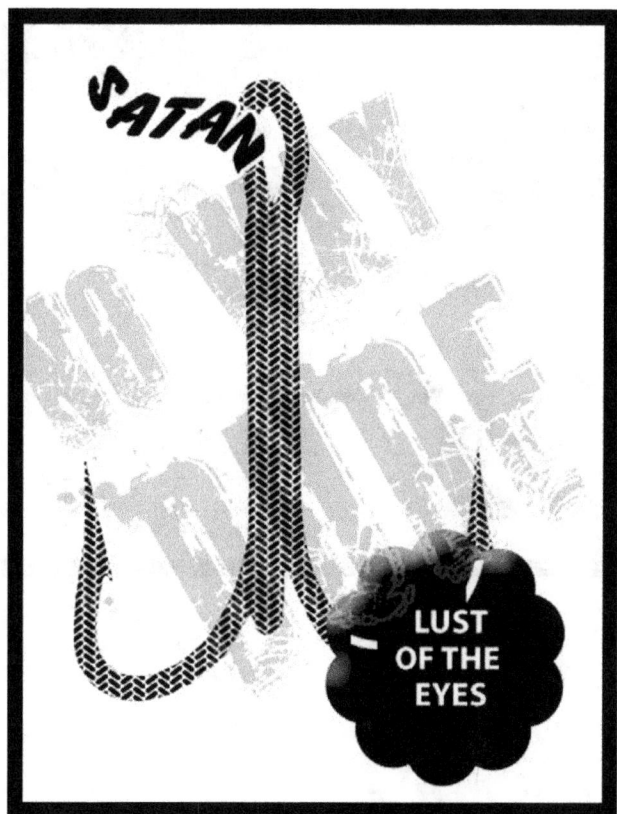

SATAN

LUST
OF THE
EYES

Two Choices in Life. Only One Demonstrates Faith in Christ, and Only by Faith in Jesus must Man be Saved...

The Self-Governed Life

SELF

Self is on the throne. Priorities and desires are directed by self, resulting in bad decisions and being outside of God's will. Jesus is not welcomed in to reign and rule as Lord.

The Christ-Governed Life

SELF

Christ is on the throne. Self yields daily to Christ. Priorities and desires are directed by Christ, resulting in harmony with God's plan.

**God grants you the Mind of Christ.
Read further in Discovery Series titles.**

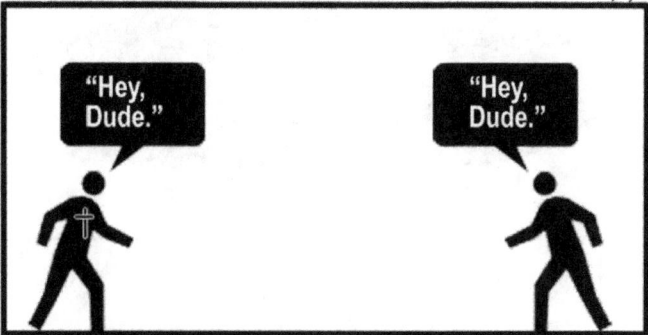

New Body, See God

Heaven

THE WORLD

WORLDLY

In bondage
to sin: idols,
sexual immorality,
impurity, envying,
living 4 self
-not 4 Jesus.

JESUS True Vine

ABIDE

OBEDIENT, LOVE JESUS, HATE SIN

Child of God,
in Jesus.
Walk with God.
Experience
True Life.

The World:
Soft on Sin.
Hard on Jesus
& Christ-Followers.
Deceived, Ripe
for Judgment,
Impenitent, Proud.

REPENT

The World:
it's Lies,
it's Disobedience,
Enemies of God.

CARNAL CHRISTIANITY

Death, Condemned,
Eternal Fire, Outer Darkness

Eternal
Separation

THE WORLD

(I used to be a...

DEATH-WALKER
(condemned zombie)

spiritually dead

JESUS

spiritually alive

alive in Christ
(justified saint)

eternal,
conscious
bliss

eternal,
conscious
death

Now I am...

REPENT,
surrender life
be born-again

"And you were dead in your trespasses and sins, in which you formerly walked according to the course of this world, according to the prince of the power of the air, of the spirit that is now working in the sons of disobedience." (Ephesians 2: 1-2)

Heaven

Glorification
New Body, See God

"Behold, I was brought forth in iniquity, And in sin my mother conceived me." (Psalms 51:5)

God's will

Jesus

"The wicked are estranged from the womb; they go astray from birth, speaking lies." (Psalms 58:3, ESV)

"and do not go on presenting the members of your body to sin as instruments of unrighteousness; but present yourselves to God as those alive from the dead, and your members as instruments of righteousness to God." (Romans: 6:13)

My will

Original

Sin

Sanctification

Justification

REPENT

Life Surrender, Re-Birth, Baptism

Eternal
Separation

Repent and turn to God, so that your sins may be wiped out.
Acts: 3:19

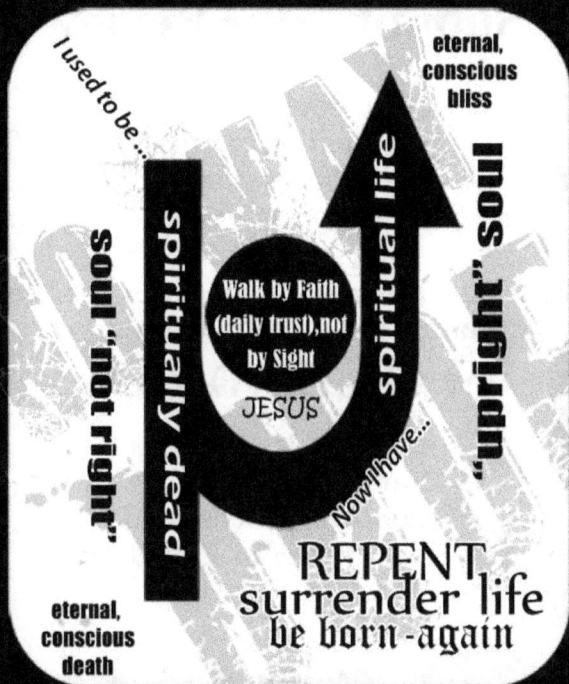

I used to be...

eternal, conscious bliss

spiritual life

spiritually dead

Soul "not right"

"upright" soul

Walk by Faith (daily trust), not by Sight

JESUS

Now I have...

REPENT surrender life be born-again

eternal, conscious death

"Look at the proud! They trust in themselves, and their lives are crooked. But the righteous will live by their faithfulness to God." (Habakkuk 2:4 NLT)

SOUL = MIND, WILL & EMOTIONS

Submit Your Review

If this book has benefited you, leaving an amazon review will assist others in benefiting from it, as well. Please consider leaving a review for this book on its Amazon page.

FINALLY: Be sure to register for blog updates and encouragement @:

www.NoWayDude.org

twitter: @NoWayDudePress
facebook: /onenewdude
YouTube: /user/nowaydudebook

Additional Resources

LINKS

1) *NoWayDude.org*
2) *jzee.TV*
3) *BibleHighlighters.TV*
4) *Evolution vs God: YouTube*
5) *JosephPrince.com*
6) *CrefloDollarMinistries.org*
7) *STR.org (&YouTube)*
8) *HisChannel.com*
9) *Bible.Is*
10) *LivingWaters.com*
11) *John's Gospel - Full Movie: YouTube*
12) *KLOVE.com (&YouTube)*

DOCS *(Google or direct site search)*

1) *Is Jesus the Only God? - marshill.com*

About the Author

Jeff Zahorsky was born in 1968 in Cleveland, Ohio to Irish and Slovak parents. A veteran of the United States Navy, Jeff served just over 6 years, primarily on Navy warships with one ground tour in Iraq. With technology as his background, Jeff holds a Certificate of Biomedicine from Boston University. It was on the flight deck of a U.S. Navy warship in Pearl Harbor, HI where he became a Christian. Jeff revels in sharing God's eternal truth through his ongoing writings.

Endnotes

[i] Ezekiel 11:19

[ii] Blue Letter Bible. "Dictionary and Word Search for metanoeō (Strong's 3340)". Blue Letter Bible. 1996-2013. 23 Aug 2013. < http://www.blueletterbible.org/lang/lexicon/lexicon.cfm?Strongs=G3340&t=NASB >

[iii] Psalm 51

[iv] Wall Street Journal. Accessed 8/23/2013 http://online.wsj.com/article/SB10001424053111903918104576502782310557332.html

[v] Driscoll, Mark

[vi] "Greek Lexicon :: G4100 (KJV)." Blue Letter Bible. Sowing Circle. Web. 2 Jan, 2014. http://www.blueletterbible.org/lang/lexicon/lexicon.cfm?Strongs=G4100&t=KJV.

[vii] James 2:19

[viii] Ezekiel 18:4

[ix] 2 Timothy 3:12

[x] Blue Letter Bible. "Dictionary and Word Search for *Satanas (Strong's 4567)*". Blue Letter Bible. 1996-2013. 24 Aug 2013. < http://www.blueletterbible.org/lang/lexicon/Lexicon.cfm?strongs=G4567 >

[xi] 1 John 1:5

[xii] Isaiah 14:9

[xiii] "Greek Lexicon :: G4357 (KJV)." Blue Letter Bible. Sowing Circle. Web. 4 Jan, 2014. <http://www.blueletterbible.org/lang/lexicon/lexicon.cfm?Strongs=G4357&t=KJV>.

[xiv] Nowaydude.org

[xv] Galatians 6:15

www.ingramcontent.com/pod-product-compliance
Lightning Source LLC
LaVergne TN
LVHW051511080426
835509LV00017B/2020